d

A guide to recent architecture

•••

Hugh Broughton
with Melanie Ashton

Madrid

A guide to recent architecture

● ● ● **ellipsis** **KÖNEMANN**

•••

Madrid: a guide to recent architecture

CREATED, EDITED AND DESIGNED BY
Ellipsis London Limited
55 Charlotte Road London EC2A 3QT
E MAIL ...@ellipsis.co.uk
WWW http://www.ellipsis.co.uk
PUBLISHED IN THE UK AND AFRICA BY
Ellipsis London Limited
SERIES EDITOR Tom Neville
EDITOR Jane Lamacraft
SERIES DESIGN Jonathan Moberly
LAYOUT Pauline Harrison

COPYRIGHT © 1997 Könemann
Verlagsgesellschaft mbH
Bonner Str. 126, D-50968 Köln
PRODUCTION MANAGER Detlev Schaper
PRINTING AND BINDING Sing Cheong
Printing Ltd
Printed in Hong Kong

ISBN 3 89508 640 1 (Könemann)
ISBN 1 899858 13 X (Ellipsis)

Hugh Broughton 1997

Contents

Introduction

Madrid is a microcosm of all Spain. On the one hand it exhibits all the trappings of a capital city: wide boulevards choked with traffic, glittering skyscrapers, crowds of Euro business people and a haze of pollution. On the other hand, it is a distinctly provincial town: elderly women dressed in black chatting on tree-shaded benches or in local bakeries, the bustle of community markets and the gossip of cafés. These contrasts permeate every aspect of modern Madrid, not least its architecture.

Madrid only came to prominence as the Spanish capital when Philip II moved his court there in 1561. At the time it was little more than a small fortress town, guarding trade routes to more prosperous centres such as Toledo and Valladolid. Right in the centre of the newly unified Spain, it provided a heart to the nation, immediately becoming a focus for migration from all over the country. The inherent cultural diversity has been a feature of the city ever since.

The contrasts in contemporary Madrileño architecture reflect these multifarious influences. Unlike Barcelona, Seville or Bilbao, Madrid has relatively few projects by foreign architects, yet its recent architecture demonstrates at least an equal willingness to absorb ideas as the regional capitals. The city remains the melting-pot of Spanish architectural thought, with projects designed by Catalans, Basques and Andalucians as well as Madrileños.

The development of modern architecture in Spain is inextricably linked to the country's political history. In 1931 the Second Republic was declared on a wave of socialist euphoria. Architecturally, this optimism was expressed by GATEPAC (Grupo de Arquitectos y Técnicos Españolos para la Arquitectura Contemporanea), the group founded in Zaragoza in 1930 which promulgated the principles of the modern movement throughout Spain. The most influential works were built in Barcelona, designed by Josep Lluís Sert, Josep Torres Clavé and Joan Subirana, but the rationalist concepts established in their Casa Bloc (1932–36) and Dispensario Antituberculoso (1934–38) permeated deep into the Madrid architectural scene. By 1936, however, Spain was plunged into a bloody civil war which left republican ideals and architecture in tatters.

The impact of Franco's dictatorship on Madrileño architecture was dichotomous. Falangist policy was strictly revisionist, drawing on ill-conceived memories of empire to assert notions of strength. One of the inevitable ways to give form to this policy was through architecture, and as a result many of the buildings constructed in the early post-war years languish in monumental allusions to history. Monstrous buildings such as the Edificio España (1953) on Plaza España or the Air Ministry at Moncloa (1957) date from this era. Strangely, such desecration had advantages 30 years on: while other cities around Europe were overrun by post-modern kitsch in the 1980s, Madrid remained relatively unblighted by the whimsical addition of pediments and pastiche. Having suffered from fascist historicism in the middle of the century, Madrileños have been keen ever since to invest in modernism, a style suited to the return to democracy and the socialist renaissance.

The seeds of present-day Madrileño modernism were sown in 1949, in the middle of the Franco era, with Francisco Cabrero and Rafael Aburto's Casa Sindical, now the Ministry of Health. It took as its source the formalism of Italian fascist design and made a clear break with the imperial style. With its tough gridded façade, this brick building stands as an icon of rationalism and the precursor of much of Madrid's contemporary architecture.

By the 1960s, Spain was in financial crisis as Franco pursued a policy of staunch introversion. Eventually, the threat of bankruptcy forced the

Madrid: a guide to recent architecture

fascists to seek funds from abroad, and for the rest of the dictatorship the country was propped up by the United States in return for air and naval bases. With the advent of political intervention, the architecture of Madrid opened its doors to the influence of internationalism.

The leaders of this change in architectural mood have remained the two most influential figures on the Madrid scene: Alejandro de la Sota and Francisco Sáenz de Oíza. De la Sota's work exemplifies the restrained minimalism of later Spanish modern architecture, often animated by only one or two dynamic elements. His competition-winning design for a local government building in Tarragona (1957) represents one of the first forays into internationalism in Spain. His gymnasium at the Maravillas school in Madrid (1960) stands out as one of the most influential Spanish buildings of the past 50 years. In contrast, Sáenz de Oíza's work is extraordinarily eclectic, constantly drawing on a panoply of references. This approach is embodied in the Torres Blancas (1968). At its best, his architecture easily surpasses the quality of its sources through its freshness and repudiation of any one particular style. In some way or other, virtually every architect now practising in Madrid has been influenced by one of these two masters, or by Rafael Moneo (himself a student of Sáenz de Oíza).

By the late 1970s, a handful of the new office buildings along the Paseo de la Castellana matched the best in Europe: the office of Bankunión (1975) by José Antonio Corrales and Ramón Molezún, and the Banco de Bilbao y Vizcaya (1980) by Sáenz de Oíza, and the Adriática building (1981) by Javier Carvajal remain as inspirational today as they were at the advent of democracy. Of all these buildings, probably the most important, however, is Rafael Moneo and Ramón Bescós' head office for Bankinter (1973), one of the first to fuse modernism with traditional Spanish idioms and the precursor of the subtle eclecticism which is so much a hall-mark of contemporary Spanish architecture; this is a building that manages to be contextual, rationalist and even decorative without departing from the tenets of modernism.

With the death of Franco in 1975 Spain moved into an era of rapid change. In 1979 the socialists swept into power in Madrid on a ticket of urban modernisation. In 1982 they won the national elections, promising change and using architecture to prove it. Economic boom, accelerated by entry into the EC in 1986, brought prosperity and an explosion of creativity, known as the Movida Madrileña. All these factors played a critical part in ensuring the diversity of the city's contemporary architecture. Unlike many other European cities which saw only a mushrooming of commercial space in the 1980s, in Madrid the construction of public facilities played the greatest role in regeneration. Whole districts of social housing were built, both on the edges of the city and in its heart. To service these new *barrios*, libraries, schools, health centres and universities were established, creating urban fabric and fostering community. Meanwhile in the commercial centre of the city, construction of offices, shops and bars was replaced in the 1990s by keynote projects such as Atocha Station, the restoration of the National Library and the Museo Thyssen-Bornemisza, and the conversion of the San Carlos hospital into the Centro de Arte Reina Sofía.

By the early 1990s the political optimism and cultural energy of the reborn nation were beginning to be exhausted. While Barcelona and Seville revelled in the international limelight of the Olympics and World Expo in 1992, Madrid's attempt at its own fiesta as European City of Culture had little impact on the infrastructure of the city, leaving behind only a handful of galleries and failing to reinvigorate the Movida. But

Madrid: a guide to recent architecture

although the economy sank and politicians became embroiled in scandal, the architecture of the capital remained intrinsically intact, still counterpoising modernity, tradition and context.

The conditions for creating modernism in Spain have remained unaffected by economic biorhythms or cultural fads and this is especially true of Madrid. Most of the architects whose work is featured in this book not only read avidly about their contemporaries and frequently pass by each other's buildings, they also work together as tutors at ETSAM, Madrid University's School of Architecture. The inevitable consequence is a cross-fertilisation of ideas, a great debate on the nature of Madrileño architecture, and an application of those elements common to modernism and the Mediterranean. In particular, the Spanish climate with its strong sunlight and fierce summers encourages flowing space, the use of patios, the breakdown of inside/outside barriers and the construction of solid, insulating masonry walls.

Spanish architecture has always placed functionalism above academic correctness, erring away from the rigidities of classicism to form informal compositions. These elements are characteristics of both modernist and traditional Mediterranean architecture. Paradoxically, many Spanish architects borrow from Scandinavian modernists such as Asplund and Aalto, who were themselves so profoundly affected by the composition and form of traditional southern European buildings. It is not surprising that the recent architecture of Madrid is modernist, traditional, contextual and eclectic – all at once.

As the socialists are replaced in the City Hall, regional government and most recently in the country as a whole by the right-wing Partido Popular under José Maria Aznar, there is more than a suggestion that commerce is beginning to overtake community as the basis of architectural commissions, posing a serious threat to Spanish modernism and to the culture of the capital. But then part of the fascination of Madrid's recent architecture is its variety. Cheek by jowl with rationalist brick housing blocks are deconstructivist offices, constructivist interiors, all the horrors of American consumerism and even the exuberance of Philippe Starck. During the height of the Movida the buzzword was vibrancy. In terms of architecture this vibrancy is born out of a cosmopolitan character still unique in Spain.

ACKNOWLEDGEMENTS

I would like to thank Tom Neville for giving me the opportunity to dig deep under the skin of Madrid's architecture; Carlos Dominguez for additional photographs; Michael Taylor for talking to me about Madrid, ferrying us out to suburban projects and making our stay such fun; Isobel Pinder for lending her computer at the last hour; Mercedes Cajal and LarsErik Falk for letting us stay in their flat in the heart of the city; Virginia Ashton for putting up with us on our return; Ronnie and Anne Broughton for their constant interest; and especially all the architects who provided such detailed information about their projects, took time to explain their work and talked about architecture so passionately.

Most of all, however, I would like to thank Mel who has worked so enthusiastically with me in producing this book. She has catalogued every project, visited every building with me, provided a constant sounding board and been the most accommodating editor. This book is as much hers as mine and it is that which has made it such fun to write.

HB December 1996

Madrid: a guide to recent architecture

Using this book

The book is divided into 16 sections, each relating to a district of Madrid. The buildings are arranged along a route around each one. Many of the projects are close together and within easy walking distance. Madrid is a relatively compact city and travel is easy. The bus, metro and suburban rail (*cercanía*) systems are very comprehensive and every project can be reached from the city centre in an hour or less. Buying a book of ten tickets reduces the cost of an individual journey by half: *billette de diez* can be bought from metro stations, and Bonobus bus tickets from tobacconists and some news-stands. Travelling by bus provides one of the best ways to orientate oneself in the city. Out of the centre the best way to visit projects is by the network of *cercanías*: most exciting are the spotless air-conditioned double-decker trains, almost worthy of an entry by themselves. All the projects in this guide are within zone B2. The best way to sort out the public transport system is to buy a city transport map from the offices of the Concorcio de Transportes de Madrid at Calle Santa Engracia 120 (metro: Rios Rosas, Line 1), or, if they have not run out, from one of the EMT kiosks (eg Puerta del Sol, Plaza de Cibeles).

All the addresses in this book are given in Spanish, and wherever a building has a specific name it is also given in Spanish to make it easier to ask directions – nonetheless it is advisable to buy a good street map from a news-stand or bookshop. Many of the projects listed have been commissioned by the *Ayuntamiento*, which is the Madrid city council, or the *Comunidad*, which is the regional government.

Inevitably, many projects had to be omitted. Wherever possible, projects of interest which have not been individually covered are mentioned at the end of descriptions of nearby or related projects. The selection included should, however, give a very clear view of the recent architecture in this exciting city.

Madrid: a guide to recent architecture

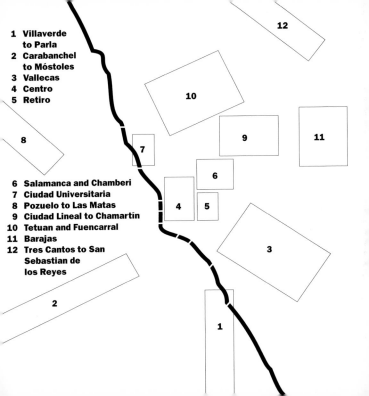

1 Villaverde
  to Parla
2 Carabanchel
  to Móstoles
3 Vallecas
4 Centro
5 Retiro

6 Salamanca and Chamberi
7 Ciudad Universitaria
8 Pozuelo to Las Matas
9 Ciudad Lineal to Chamartín
10 Tetuan and Fuencarral
11 Barajas
12 Tres Cantos to San
   Sebastian de
   los Reyes

Villaverde to Parla

Republica del Brasil School

As an international lecturer, critic and professor at ETSAM, Alberto Campo Baeza has emerged as one of the most influential Spanish architects of recent years. His architecture is minimalist, contextual and, above all, economic.

Facing on to a gridded area of tree-lined streets and single-storey workers' houses, the three-storey building provides additional classrooms for a school. The site for the extension was restricted both by planning laws and the building programme, yet it achieves great eloquence.

Corridors on the north are set behind a brick wall separated from an older school building by only a few metres. Small inset windows emphasise the wall's fortress-like quality. Classrooms are arranged in a line and face south, opening out to the playground and the sun. The hall is the centre of the linear building, breaking through the brick walls with a glass-block cylinder, its interior bathed in diffuse light. Within this cylindrical volume, the stair is clamped between white-painted concrete frames. Landings overlook the triple-height space, lit behind by clear glazed rooflights which cap the cylinder.

Unfortunately, pupils and staff do not seem to have shown the school the same respect as the international architectural press. An important piece of modern architecture is being desecrated by lack of maintenance, the scourge of public buildings in Spain.

ADDRESS Avenida de los Fueros, San Fermín, 28041 Madrid
CLIENT Ministerio de Educacion y Ciencia
TECHNICAL ARCHITECT Miguel Mesas
AREA 1800 square metres COST 90 million pesetas
METRO *cercanía* to Orcasitas (C5) then bus 78 BUS 23, 78, 123
ACCESS school hours

Alberto Campo Baeza 1985

Alberto Campo Baeza 1985

El Espinillo Health Centre

The health centre faces on to a large, neglected space at the heart of a new *barrio*. The building is divided by a double-height reception lobby. Administrative areas are arranged in a two-storey tower enclosed on one side by an undulating skin of galvanised corrugated steel. The tower rests on a rectangular slate-clad base. Windows set into the rendered side of the tower fill the top floor with sunlight. Treatment rooms are to the south on two floors. A waiting area is sandwiched between the rooms, glazed to the south, offering views and catching daylight.

The reception area is glazed both to the street and the private garden to the west, visually separating the two parts of the health centre. A circular lift shaft and open steel stair give access to the basement and upper levels, filling the reception with activity. The centre is much lower than the surrounding housing blocks, so the stairs, lifts, freeform tower and a multi-use room are arranged on the roof, as if a fifth elevation.

Starting from a relatively simple brief, Isasi and Pieltáin have created a building of great contrasts. The hierarchical design of elevations responds both to aspect and context. In the absence of any other public facilities, the *barrio* has gained a focus for its community.

ADDRESS Avenida Orovilla/Avenida Felicidad, 28041 Madrid
CLIENT Insalud
TECHNICAL ARCHITECT Mariano Caballero
STRUCTURAL ENGINEER Victor Rios
AREA 1659 square metres COST 197 million pesetas
METRO *cercanía* to Villaverde Bajo (C3, C4) then bus 123 BUS 123
ACCESS Monday to Friday 9.00–21.00

Villaverde to Parla

Justo Isasi and Alberto Pieltáin 1991–93

Justo Isasi and Alberto Pieltáin 1991–93

San Cristóbal de los Ángeles Health Centre

San Cristóbal de los Ángeles is one of the tougher *barrios* on the edges of Madrid. Many of the housing blocks here were built before the advent of democracy and provide only cramped accommodation. Local action groups are vociferous, the crime rate is high and substance abuse is a serious problem. Against this background, the health centre plays a crucial socio-iconographic role and provides a focus for the community.

A regular grid of columns supports a steel roof, enabling floors to adopt different forms beneath. The public entrance is clearly placed on the corner, turning access through 90 degrees. This opens up the building both to the derelict open land in front and the narrow street at the side. Positioning the main entrance facing on to the side road contributes to a safer environment.

Each floor is planned around the central atrium. Waiting areas are sited next to it, with treatment rooms around the perimeter. Administrative offices are divided from treatment rooms by a concrete service wall containing stairs, lifts, toilets and storage. As each floor plan changes, so does the form of the atrium and the main stair, elevating the components of the building into sculptural elements in their own right. The oxidised steel façade provides a complete contrast to the crumbling brick and blockwork of neighbouring buildings.

ADDRESS Calle Benimamet, Villaverde, 28021 Madrid
CLIENT Insalud
STRUCTURAL ENGINEER Alfonso del Rio
AREA 3000 square metres COST 400 million pesetas
METRO *cercanía* to Los Ángeles (C3) BUS 59, 79
ACCESS open

Villaverde to Parla

Sebastián Araujo and Jaime Nadal 1989–94

Sebastián Araujo and Jaime Nadal 1989–94

Fernando de los Rios Students' Residence

This dramatic wedge-shaped brick building guards the entry into Getafe from the Carretera de Toledo. It is the latest addition to the Universidad Carlos III, whose campus was also designed by Rodríguez de Partearroyo (see page 24).

A copper-clad fin marks the apex of the wedge, dividing triangular concrete balconies. From eight storeys at the head of the block, the façades reduce to three at the back. The entrance slices across the triangular plan form to give access from the university and the nearby train station. Bedsit apartments are arranged along the perimeters, each with a balcony. In the centre of the wedge a glass and concrete roof covering the café and common room allows natural light into the heart of the building.

At ground level, double-height retail units face on to the street, separated by stone-clad piers. Above, balconies to apartments are divided by vertical glazed slots to access corridors. The windows to apartments are splayed at 45 degrees to the façade to reduce solar penetration, making the balconies look like dark recesses set into the brickwork. The rear elevation is as sculptural as the sides, with banks of balconies and extract flues descending in an ever-widening cascade.

ADDRESS Avenida de las Ciudades 1, Getafe, 28903 Madrid
CLIENT Universidad Carlos III and Instituto de la Vivienda de Madrid
SIZE 200 apartments
METRO *cercanía* to Las Margaritas Universidad (C4)
ACCESS open

Francisco Rodríguez de Partearroyo 1994

Francisco Rodríguez de Partearroyo 1994

Universidad Carlos III

The Carlos III university occupies a former army barracks, extending the complex and introducing a series of major interventions. It is symmetrical about the Patio de las Promociones, a rectangular tree-shaded space full of activity. The plaza is surrounded by the original rendered, pantile-roofed buildings which have been carefully conserved. Only the cafeteria has been perceptibly extended into the plaza with a virtuoso hi-tech assembly of curved glass, expressed structure and steel sunshades.

To the east of the plaza a similar element containing a semicircular assembly hall links the old and new buildings of the university offices. The original bridge link between the two parallel buildings has been enclosed by a glazed pavilion and now includes stairs and a waiting area.

Brick-clad frames, glazed façades, steel sunshades and black metal-work are consistently used as cladding. Facing out of the campus the façades are more muscular, with lower levels set back behind brick piers and capped by an attic storey of student accommodation. Internally, white marble floors are combined with Oregon-pine-clad walls in class-rooms and offices, and fairfaced brickwork elsewhere.

ADDRESS Calle Madrid 126, Getafe, 28903 Madrid
CLIENT Universidad Carlos III and Comunidad de Madrid
TECHNICAL ARCHITECTS Antonio Rodríguez Romero and Fernando Vasco Hidalgo
STRUCTURAL ENGINEERS Building Laboratory at ETSAM
SERVICES ENGINEER Rafael Urculo
AREA 50,000 square metres COST 7800 million pesetas
METRO *cercanía* to Las Magaritas Universidad (C4)
ACCESS open

Francisco Rodríguez de Partearroyo 1988–90

Francisco Rodríguez de Partearroyo 1988–90

Co-operative Housing

For 15 years, Ruíz Barbarín worked in Gabriel Allende's studio, but he now has a flourishing practice of his own. This co-operative housing project shows off his adroitness, particularly in the context of the Swiss chalet-style housing that litters the Getafe district of El Casar.

The square development has a hard outer skin punctured by small square windows and louvred balconies to kitchens, bedrooms and drying areas. Corners on the west side and cores popping up above the tiled pitched roof are finished in grey render, compounding the austerity.

There are two entrances at the east corners, one for cars and another for pedestrians, slicing through the block on the diagonal. The skewed façades are yellow rendered with expressed joints at floor levels, steel channel cornices and a vertical splayed window poking out from stairs. The entrances reveal a beautifully planted courtyard furnished with a small playground, benches, lighting and table-tennis table. Like an oasis set in the arid suburban landscape, the gardens give a focus to the building and encourage a sense of community. As a result, they are carefully tended by residents and constantly active, filled with children and chatting adults.

The elevations surrounding the garden are rendered, with balconies to living rooms and expressed stair cores. Protruding glass boxes define entrances; the cores above are grey rendered, contrasting with the yellow of the flats and broken up by horizontal slit windows to the stair landings.

ADDRESS Avenida Don Juan de Bourbon 1, Getafe, 28903 Madrid
CLIENT Cooperativa de Jovenes – Getafe 92
AREA 13,200 square metres COST 960 million pesetas
METRO *cercanía* to Las Magaritas Universidad (C4) BUS 447
ACCESS none

Antonio Ruíz Barbarín 1994

Antonio Ruíz Barbarín 1994

Casa Consistorial

Parla is a dormitory town with few public buildings except the church and the old town hall. Junquera/Pérez-Pita's design draws these important elements together with the site for the new Casa Consistorial.

Their building contains municipal offices, a police station, public library, council chamber, exhibition space, staff areas and underground parking. Politicians' offices have been retained in the old white-washed town hall opposite.

Offices are positioned on three floors behind the Colmenar limestone façade which follows the curve of Calle de Olivio. At street level, the façade is broken, giving views of the church from the plaza and creating an entrance into the offices. From a triple-height entrance hall a broad stair descends, bordered by a glazed curtain wall, to an exhibition area and the council chamber. The cylindrical chamber frames the entrance to the square from Calle del Hospital, providing a pivot to the organisation of the project. Internally, clerestory light fills the upper part of the chamber which is finished in galvanised corrugated steel. Externally, the corrugated steel curiously blocks out square openings punched into the cylinder just below the clerestory glazing.

Parallel to the stairs a narrow two-storey staff pavilion reduces the scale to match that of the older buildings around the plaza. It is connected to the main block by a bridge at first-floor level. A monopitch roof oversails the different structures, drawing them all together under one umbrella and shading them from the sun.

ADDRESS Plaza de la Constitucion 1, Parla, 28980 Madrid
CLIENT Ayuntamiento de Parla
METRO *cercanía* to Parla (C4)
ACCESS entrance area only

Jerónimo Junquera and Estanislao Pérez-Pita 1986–92

Jerónimo Junquera and Estanislao Pérez-Pita 1986–92

Carabanchel to Móstoles

General Ricardos Housing 1

The design of this housing project provides a reinterpretation of the traditional architecture of Carabanchel, once a summer retreat for royalty in an area of smallholdings. The neighbouring old buildings are mostly two storeys and grouped around internal courtyards.

Along the busy General Ricardos a three-storey block incorporates retail units at street level, while elsewhere the development contains only two-storey housing. Each of the terraced housing units is arranged in an L-shape. At entry level a living room and kitchen look on to a double-height terrace. Bedrooms are grouped around this external atrium on the level above. The bathrooms, internal stairs and services are arranged along a central spine which emerges at roof level, clad in travertine and punctured by ventilation grilles. The houses are arranged in a U-shape around large courtyards, bringing identity and community to the block.

Following their ground-breaking brick housing schemes in Palomeras in the early 1980s, the Casas brothers and Lorenzo have more recently investigated alternative elevational treatments such as render and precast-concrete panels. The concrete cornice has also become a recurring feature in their work, though in this project, caged-in terraces strike the dominant note in the elevational design. These provide protection from vandalism and break-ins and offer a sense of enclosure. The continued cornice line and concrete column at each recess increase this protective quality.

ADDRESS Calle General Ricardos 191–195, Calle Eugenia de Montijo 24–40, 28025 Madrid
CLIENT Empresa Municipal de la Vivienda
METRO Carabanchel (line 5) BUS 34
ACCESS none

Manuel de las Casas, Ignacio de las Casas, Jaime Lorenzo 1988–90

Manuel de las Casas, Ignacio de las Casas, Jaime Lorenzo 1988–90

General Ricardos Housing 2

This competition-winning design meets very particular planning requirements for each face of an urban block, and elegantly connects to an existing building. Along General Ricardos the building follows the taut curve of the street with an arcade of small shops at ground level and housing above. In the afternoon, shadows from the brick piers create a changing faceted pattern on the paving of the arcade. The block facing on to the street slots on to a taller four-storey block behind, which in turn faces on to a green and tranquil garden.

On the other three sides, two-storey houses with pitched tile roofs are arranged around the garden in terraces. These relate in scale and appearance to the neighbouring *pueblo* houses which made up most of the village of Carabanchel before it was absorbed into the city.

Detailing – such as the slot window separating the three- and four-storey elements – is very simple and only rarely expressive. Nevertheless, enormous variety has been created by plan and section within a harmonious whole and on an extremely tight budget.

The brick housing to the south on either side of General Ricardos was designed by Vázquez de Castro and Iñiquez de Onzoño (1981–86). The dominant caged balconies offer a threatening metaphor for the nearby Carabanchel prison.

ADDRESS Calle General Ricardos 199–205, Calle Monseñor Oscar Romero 32–34, 28025 Madrid
CLIENT Empresa Municipal de la Vivienda
AREA 5953 square metres COST 171 million pesetas
METRO Carabanchel (line 5) BUS 34
ACCESS none

Fernando Torres and Ernesto Muntaner 1991

Guareña Housing

Of the co-operative housing projects west of Avenida de los Poblados, this development of two facing linear blocks is undoubtedly the most interesting. To break down the volume of the 180-metre building, 104 apartments are placed in six distinct 21 x 21 metre towers which rise above a full-length plinth containing commercial units. The first four floors of housing in each block are identical, with four apartments per floor, each with a double aspect. A patio brings light and air into the heart of the building. First-floor apartments have access to a roof garden between the towers. Every window and door is standardised to reduce costs. At the two ends of the development the towers are a further three storeys tall. The square brick form of the lower levels is cut away to a rendered cylinder on the east and west façades, although the flat brick plane continues on the north and south sides.

Through a series of housing projects, these architects have developed themes of overlaying geometries. These break up mass and introduce order and hierarchy to large developments. Residents can stand in the road and point to their own flat, recognisable by its form and specific exposure of render or brick. Looking at some of the neighbouring developments, this seems quality that is all too rare.

ADDRESS Calle Guareña 2–12, 28024 Madrid
CLIENT Los Poblados 18.000 SCL
TECHNICAL ARCHITECTS Vicente Arenas and Beatriz Torralba
AREA 21,000 square metres COST 932 million pesetas
METRO Empalme (line 10), Aluche (lines 5, 10, C5)
BUS 36, H
ACCESS none

Alvarez-Sala, Rubio Carvajal, Ruíz-Larrea 1993–94

Alvarez-Sala, Rubio Carvajal, Ruíz-Larrea 1993–94

Polígono C Housing 1

The Polígono C development in Carabanchel is an experiment in low-density villa-type social housing. The L-shaped site overlooks the Parque de Las Tres Cruces. Three architectural practices were selected to design blocks of housing and together established ground rules for the masterplan: three-storey blocks with four apartments per floor; views over the park; blocks which open on to the surrounding paths and streets; and improved safety (see pages 40 and 42).

Cruz and Ortiz have adopted a linear model for the ten northernmost blocks, in contrast to the centralised model of the other two architects. The blocks face into well-maintained gardens. The ends step down, enabling a mix of two-, three- and four-bed units each with its own outside space. At ground level the four-bed units facing the gardens have their own terrace, while the three-bed units facing on to the street have gardens enclosed by walls. Bedrooms and living spaces are arranged around the perimeter with bathrooms and kitchens in a central spine.

The cantilevered concrete roofs and varied planes are reminiscent of inter-war Dutch architecture. Facing into the development, the interlocking balconies at each end cascade down into the gardens, the receding planes animating the formal brick façade. This approach brings life to the entrances, making them busy and safe.

ADDRESS Calle Arbol del Cielo 1–9, Calle de la Vidauba 10–18, 28044 Madrid
CLIENT Instituto de la Vivienda de Madrid
TECHNICAL ARCHITECT Carlos Ruíz de la Escalera
AREA 12,475 square metres COST 422 million pesetas
METRO *cercanía* to Fanjul (C5), Aluche (lines 5, 10, C5) BUS 17, 34
ACCESS none

Antonio Cruz and Antonio Ortiz 1986–89

Antonio Cruz and Antonio Ortiz 1986–89

Polígono C Housing 2

At the corner of Polígono C, the ten brick blocks designed by the Basque architect Luis Peña Ganchegui each focuses on a central patio. This is covered by a distinctive pyramidal rooflight, raised above the clay pantile roof by steel trusses, enabling air to circulate through the heart of the building. Double-aspect living rooms are positioned on corners, with bedrooms in between. Bathrooms and kitchens surround the patio, filling the central space with noise and cooking smells.

The brick elevations are unimpressive, though they are enlivened both by the floating rooflight and the ornate steel structure at cornice level which lifts the roof above the block in a faintly grand gesture. The buildings are organised around a grid of tree-planted pathways furnished with benches. At the right angle of the L-shaped site, housing is replaced by a community centre which faces on to a small plaza.

Although the plan helps to foster a sense of community, the overall layout does not claim the external spaces with the same vigour as the two neighbouring schemes (see pages 38 and 42). There is no clearly defined semi-public space and as a result residents do not feel a sense of ownership of the external areas.

ADDRESS Calle Vidauba 20–24, Calle Garapalo 2–8, 28044 Madrid
CLIENT Instituto de la Vivienda de Madrid
SIZE ten blocks plus community building
METRO *cercanía* to Fanjul (C5), Aluche (lines 5, 10, C5) BUS 17, 34
ACCESS none

Luis Peña Ganchegui 1987–89

Luis Peña Ganchegui 1987–89

Polígono C Housing 3

This scheme by the Casas brothers and Jaime Lorenzo bears many similarities to the neighbouring blocks designed by Peña Ganchegui (see page 40): flats are arranged around a central space with double-aspect living rooms on corners and service spaces facing on to a patio; the central rooflight is lifted up to aid air circulation and the blocks all measure 20 x 20 metres. Here, however, the articulation is very different. Corners are cut away to orientate groups of four blocks on to small raised circular plazas. This creates a sense of community not only within the blocks, but between blocks too. The success of such a simple concept is immediately apparent in the manicured flower beds and clean paving, all maintained daily by the tenants. The curved cut-back entrance leads directly on to the patio, where the stair criss-crosses first one way, then the other, providing sculptural expression to the void. Each block contains two four-bed units, seven three-bed units and two two-bed units. The cylinder on top houses stores and encloses the rooflight, its curved form creating a compositional tension with the square of the main block below.

The building is capped by a concrete cornice and finished in render to contrast with its brick-faced neighbours. Incised lines in the render hint at floor and ceiling levels behind.

ADDRESS Calle Garapalo 10–18, Calle Arbol del Cielo 19–25, 28044 Madrid
CLIENT Instituto de la Vivienda de Madrid
SIZE ten blocks of 11 apartments each
METRO *cercanía* to Fanjul (C5), Aluche (lines 5, 10, C5) BUS 17, 34
ACCESS none

Manuel de las Casas, Ignacio de las Casas, Jaime Lorenzo 1986–89

Manuel de las Casas, Ignacio de las Casas, Jaime Lorenzo 1986–89

La Latina Library

With its clearly organised and autonomous architecture, the library dominates this important corner site. Its isosceles triangle shape allows a simplified system of control around a central desk. A void lets controlled daylight permeate right into the heart of the building.

Access to the library runs along one side of the triangle with entrances on both Rafael Finat and José de Cadalso. Lifts and stairs climb up small voids to the side of the circulation spine. At ground level, the bull-nosed end on to Rafael Finat contains a lecture theatre, its curve providing a smooth transition at the acute angle. The clear, almost diagrammatic organisation is reflected in the elevations. The curved circulation core is brick clad with inlet glass-block lenses which throw twinkles of light on to the stairs. The library is more refined, clad in 30-millimetre-thick blocks of limestone with deeply recessed strip glazing. Aluminium sunshades keep glare off the desks which are positioned around the perimeter of the library.

The surrounding area has been carefully landscaped with gentle grass terraces and seating, creating a tranquil resting place.

ADDRESS Calle Rafael Finat/Calle José de Cadalso, 28044 Madrid
CLIENT Comunidad de Madrid
STRUCTURAL ENGINEER Alfonso Gómez Gaite
MECHANICAL AND ELECTRICAL ENGINEER Manuel López Acosta
AREA 3298 square metres COST 350 million pesetas
METRO *cercanía* to Fanjul (c5), Aluche (lines 5, 10, c5), then bus 17
BUS 17
ACCESS during opening hours

Carabanchel to Móstoles

Francisco Rodríguez de Partearroyo 1990–92

Francisco Rodríguez de Partearroyo 1990–92

Alcalde Bartolomé Gonzalez Health Centre

Set in gardens in the old part of Móstoles, a dormitory town which has mushroomed in the last 20 years, the health centre is organised in single-storey elements crowding around a double-storey cylindrical block.

The building focuses on a central courtyard. This introspection is emphasised by a lead-clad monopitched roof which tilts away from the park and towards the courtyard. A drug clinic with its own square patio forms one of the single-storey elements, with staff areas and social services offices in the other.

A stair curves round the outer wall of the cylinder, climbing over the reception. Consulting rooms are arranged around the outside, with waiting areas overlooking the courtyard. On both levels, beams are exposed to the ceiling like bicycle spokes.

Externally, the form is dominated by the geometrical superimposition of square on circle. On the upper level, precast concrete planks compress strip windows against the stone rubble base. Ground-floor windows are larger and square, protected by metal grilles. In contrast, the single-storey elements are rendered, with slotted windows set against larger grilled openings.

ADDRESS Calle de la Independencia 8, Móstoles, 28931 Madrid
CLIENT Insalud
TECHNICAL ARCHITECTS J G Delgado and J A Valdés
STRUCTURAL ENGINEER J M Fernandez
AREA 2000 square metres COST 250 million pesetas
METRO *cercanía* to Móstoles (C5) BUS 519, 520, 521, 524, 525, 526
ACCESS Monday to Friday 8.30–21.00; Saturday 9.00–17.00

Carlos Puente and Víctor López Cotelo 1990–94

Vallecas

Arroyo de la Media Legua Housing

There is huge variety in the social housing stock of Madrid. Increasingly, architects are looking at different ways to create identity, hierarchy and form within the parameters of sophisticated and specific briefs. This project resolves many of these issues, although, like so many public buildings, poor maintenance is taking a heavy toll on its appearance.

Bedrooms are on the north side, behind a gentle curve which cantilevers over the pavement the maximum 1 metre permitted by planning regulations. Kitchens and living rooms look south; this façade, which features balconies, is more open and animated. Perforated aluminium cladding protects access stairs, ducting and drying rooms. Ground-floor apartments have their own protected external space and entrance, and the top two floors are reorganised into maisonettes. At each end, kitchens are orientated through 90 degrees to prevent blind elevations. The building is capped by a 10-centimetre cantilevered concrete cornice, a recurring detail in Araujo and Nadal's work.

Looking around at the neighbouring buildings it is easy to understand the importance of applying basic principles to housing design. While many of them have been well designed by reputable architects, they lack certain important criteria apparent in this block, particularly the animated end elevations, hierarchy in façades and the visual cap at the top of the building.

ADDRESS Calle Arroyo de la Media Legua 59–67, 28030 Madrid
CLIENT Empresa Municipal de la Vivienda
STRUCTURAL ENGINEER Alfonso del Rio SERVICES ENGINEER Manuel Peña
AREA 8500 square metres COST 360 million pesetas
METRO Estrella, Vinateros (line 9) BUS 71, 113
ACCESS none

Vallecas

Sebastián Araujo and Jaime Nadal 1988–90

Sebastián Araujo and Jaime Nadal 1988–90

M30 Housing 1

This is one of Madrid's most controversial projects and, frankly, one of the most outrageous. Yet it was designed by Francisco Sáenz de Oíza, the architect of such inspiring buildings as the Torres Blancas (1968), the Banco de Bilbao y Vizcaya (1980) and the Atlantic Centre for Modern Art in Las Palmas (1989). The sinuous block contains 346 housing units intended for some of the poorest Madrid families, former residents of the appalling shanty towns which pockmark the outer edges of the city. Many of the original tenants moved in for only a short time before selling their apartments on the black market to less needy families, thus destroying the *raison d'être* of the project.

The snail-like shape was predetermined by the general plan for this area, but the articulation is unmistakably Oíza's. The relentless brick external elevation punctured by tiny squares is hostile and unnecessary. Even though the building sits on the banks of the M30 motorway, the problem of noise penetration could have been dealt with much more subtly, as it has been in other schemes in similar situations. Here the façade is more imposing than a prison and does nothing to inspire a sense of homeliness among the already beleaguered residents. The only modulation in the elevation is the change in height down to the main entrance.

The internal elevations are the complete opposite, but just as outrageous. Sculpturally, they express the organisation of the apartments, each of which has a lower living level and an upper bedroom level. Most of the units have three bedrooms, with the third bedroom overlooking a partly double-height terrace. On the fourth and fifth floors, the units have four bedrooms and therefore only single-storey balconies which form a cornice around the inner face of the development. Decoratively, the inner elevation stoops to the patronising with garish, gaudy and ill-conceived post-modern motifs daubed on to a yellow background. The introversion

Francisco Sáenz de Oíza 1986–89

Vallecas

Francisco Sáenz de Oíza 1986–89

of the plan was designed to create security in the central space, though the playgrounds have long since been destroyed and children are forced to play among weeds and parched earth. The car parks at semi-basement level are empty and ransacked by vandals.

Oíza's work never fails to attract attention. There are few Madrileños who do not know this building, which they call 'El Huevo' ('The Egg'). Unfortunately, the dynamism of this illustrious architect has here been seriously misdirected.

ADDRESS Calle Félix Rodríguez de la Fuente 3–73, Calle Doctor Garcia Tapia 1–23, 28030 Madrid
CLIENT Instituto de la Vivienda de Madrid
SIZE 346 housing units
METRO Estrella (line 9) BUS 71
ACCESS to external communal areas only

Vallecas

Francisco Sáenz de Oíza 1986–89

Francisco Sáenz de Oíza 1986–89

M30 Housing 2

The U-shaped plan of this housing block curves with the M30 slip road into Avenida de García Tapia. Facing on to the motorway, the elevation exudes strength and offers protection. Brick blocks cantilever out from a solid base like buttresses; windows are positioned in the sides so that the principal façade is left blank. The top floor is set back and commands panoramic views over the city. Away from the motorway, the façades are plainer, responding to a less hostile context.

The inner face of the U offers a rigorous version of current Madrileño rationalist architecture. Brick-clad stair and lift towers provide order, dividing up the rendered elevations. Ground-floor flats open on to an enclosed private patio, while all the other apartments have balconies facing on to the poorly maintained communal garden. The top two floors are designed as maisonettes, although, like most of the flats, they have three bedrooms.

Along the straighter sides of the development, the top floor is set back from the gardens and steps out towards the exterior. At the curve, this floor is set back from the motorway to cantilever over the seventh-floor balcony below. Bedrooms face out of the development and living areas face inwards.

ADDRESS Avenida Corregidor Diego de Valderrábano 37–77, 28030 Madrid
CLIENT Empresa Municipal de la Vivienda
AREA 35,600 square metres
COST 1600 million pesetas
METRO Estrella (line 9) BUS 71
ACCESS none

José Maria García de Paredes 1988–91

José Maria García de Paredes 1988–91

Sierra Elvira Housing

Two asymmetrical blocks are centred on a small, shaded plaza to make a symmetrical whole. On the west side, they look across wasteland to the junction of the M30 with the Avenida del Mediterráneo, the motorway to Valencia. The development contains 86 dwellings, with a mix of two-, three- and four-bed units, and two floors of basement parking. Each block is planned with kitchens and bathrooms facing either into an internal lightwell or out through side elevations. Living rooms and bedrooms face out towards the motorways or on to Calle Sierra Elvira.

The rationalist elevation on to Calle Sierra Elvira is rendered above a brick base and punctured by a regular grid of windows. It does not seem out of place at the end of a street made up of similarly rationalist buildings, all heavily influenced by the Italian Aldo Rossi.

The west elevation exhibits much greater plasticity, with a series of planes, solids, voids and splays creating a painterly composition. Continuous protruding concrete sills emphasise horizontality. A pergola at roof level protects a long balcony which, in a gymnastic detail, cantilevers to provide a dynamic look-out.

Many of the elements in this block are developed from ideas first promulgated by Vázquez Consuegra in his housing scheme on Calle Ramon y Cajal in Seville (1984–87), in particular the subtle transformation of elements such as balconies into cornices, and the artistically abstract composition of elevations.

ADDRESS Calle Sierra Elvira 21–27, 28038 Madrid
CLIENT Empresa Municipal de la Vivienda
AREA 10,380 square metres COST 338 million pesetas
METRO Puente de Vallecas (line 1), then bus 113 or 8 BUS 141, 113, 8
ACCESS none

Vallecas

Guillermo Vázquez Consuegra 1988–91

Vallecas

Guillermo Vázquez Consuegra 1988–91

M30 Housing 3

The industrial appearance of this competition-winning housing scheme sets it apart from other similar projects. Abalos and Herreros worked with Salvador Pérez Arroyo before establishing their own practice and inherited his interest in the application of technology.

The building sits on a concrete plinth, with floors above clad in silver-profiled steel sheets. The top floor is set back from the motorway elevation and finished with a curved roof. Balconies facing on to the M30 are fully glazed, like integral conservatories. Open drying areas are set behind the metal cladding, perforated to help air circulation. The entire east elevation appears hermetically sealed from the noise and traffic.

A separate semicircular three-storey block to the north changes scale as the block turns into Calle de Nuevo Baztan. It contains maisonettes with storage and garages below. The protruding glass *miradores*, cantilevered concrete canopy and curved form combine to give a more dynamic and sculptural appearance than the linear neighbour. Entry into all the units is via steel and glass lobbies protruding from the west elevation.

The project acts as a metaphor for the mixed residential and industrial buildings which make up this area. Whether or not it proves a justifiable approach will be borne out in time, though the notion of superimposing an industrial skin on a residential body already seems contentious.

ADDRESS Calle de Valderribas 86, 28007 Madrid
CLIENT Empresa Municipal de la Vivienda
AREA 6000 square metres, 52 units COST 292 million pesetas
METRO Puente de Vallecas (line 1)
BUS 8, 10, 24, 37, 54, 56, 57, 140, 141, E
ACCESS none

Vallecas

Iñaki Abalos and Juan Herreros 1989–92

Iñaki Abalos and Juan Herreros 1989–92

Payaso Fofó Sports Centre

The site of the sports centre is restricted, so facilities have had to be planned over six floors. Squash courts are positioned behind the concrete wall facing on to Calle Payaso Fofó. The glass wall above, which is structurally silicone-bonded to a frame of steel channels, contrasts with the stark concrete structure of the adjacent Rayo Vallecano football stadium. The glass detailing of the façade is innocently crude, setting the mood for the rest of the building. Small stainless steel clips restrain the glass in case the adhesive silicone fails.

Behind the glass there are plenty of allusions to hi-tech: exposed ductwork, folded steel-plate stairs and lots of visible steel trusses. The translucent roof over the indoor basketball court is supported on a 6.6-metre gridded steel structure. Below, the swimming pool takes up another huge volume, with views out to the south-east. On all floors, the space next to the glass wall is used for circulation, no doubt because heat build-up would prevent too much exertion in these areas.

The triple-height entrance lobby is finished in rough, exposed concrete and visibly welded mild steel balustrades. Industrial details complement the concept of 'pumping iron'. The short south-west façade is unnecessarily blind. Opening up the ramps and stairs behind would have been more consistent with the basic architectural approach.

Pérez Arroyo also designed the Madrid Planetarium (1984–87) in the Parque Tierno Galván, an even earlier investigation into high-tech.

ADDRESS Calle Payaso Fofó, 28018 Madrid
CLIENT Ayuntamiento de Madrid
AREA 5800 square metres COST 150 million pesetas
METRO Portazgo (line 1) BUS 10, 57, 103
ACCESS open

Salvador Pérez Arroyo 1986–88

Vallecas

Salvador Pérez Arroyo 1986–88

Vallecas

Palomeras Housing

Julio Cano Lasso is one of Madrid's great modern masters and a leading exponent of brickwork building. His influence on many younger architects has been far-reaching.

With its finger-like bands of brick balconies, the muscular arched entrance facing into public gardens, and the pronounced rounded prow at the junction of Calle de Pedro Laborde and Calle de Guillermo Pingarron, this building bears inevitable comparisons with early twentieth-century Viennese architecture. Many of the details stand up to the same comparison: lights bear traces of Josef Hoffman and the steel gates to the entrance mimic art nouveau metalwork.

The gardens, designed by Manolo Paredes, overlay informal landscaping on a rationalist grid. The parallel paths are pleasantly shaded and the small pond is refreshing. At lunchtime, evenings and weekends, the residents of Palomeras fill the little park, taking a gentle *paseo* or chatting as they sit on the simple but ingenious concrete and steel benches.

Nearby are two developments designed by Fernando Prats and Alfredo Villanueva. At Calle de Pedro Laborde 57–69, huge brick piers march around the superblock (1988–92). The twin buildings at Avenida de Palomeras 153–155 (1989) face Cano Lasso's scheme. They enclose well-maintained and shady communal gardens.

ADDRESS Avenida de Palomeras 145–149, Calle de Pedro Laborde 27–41, 28038 Madrid
CLIENT Instituto de la Vivienda de Madrid
METRO Alto del Arenal (line 1) BUS 10
ACCESS none

Vallecas

Julio Cano Lasso 1988-91

Julio Cano Lasso 1988-91

Buenos Aires Housing

Looking south from here into the fields, one is reminded that this is the very edge of Madrid. It is also a transition point between the redevelopments of south-east Palomeras and the recent gridded development of Madrid Sur, the massive housing project masterplanned by Antonio Vázquez de Castro (1987–95). In this light, the appearance of a block designed like a Castilian fortress seems wholly appropriate.

Despite the steep sloping site, the roof-line is constant, exaggerating the robustness of the flat, pale brick façades. At ground level, retail units and bars are slotted into portals, bringing life to the street. Above are two floors of square openings to the apartments behind. Cantilevered steel balconies to top-floor living rooms cast shadows on to the brickwork. A gated entrance set in the long façade leads into a central courtyard which is divided into three on the upper levels by two parallel bridges of accommodation. Arcades combine with the pebble-finished patio to create a modern reinterpretation of a traditional Spanish building. The colour of drying washing adds to the atmosphere.

Detailing is typically minimalist. Particularly intriguing are the steel doors which give access from the street and which are angled at 45 degrees to the façade. The contrast in Bayón's work between swathes of plain brickwork and immaculate steelwork detailing makes for a seductive form of modernism.

ADDRESS Avenida de Buenos Aires, 28038 Madrid
CLIENT Instituto de la Vivienda de Madrid
TECHNICAL ARCHITECT José Angel Azañedo
AREA 55 housing units, 10 retail units COST 294 million pesetas
METRO Buenos Aires (line 1) BUS 10
ACCESS none

Vallecas

Mariano Bayón 1988–90

Mariano Bayón 1988–90

Puerto del Milagro Housing

In 1992, Martínez-Lapeña and Torres designed one of the most exuberant housing schemes in Barcelona's Olympic Village. This project shares some of the same qualities. The tower's undulating brick façade, coronated roof line and open inner face also bear witness to the influence of the Catalan modernist José Antonio Coderch.

The development provides accommodation for young people in a low-rise block, terraced housing and 15-storey tower. The tower stands on a plinth, the highest point in the area, commanding dramatic views over all Madrid. Directly below, the grid of Madrid Sur tails off into agricultural land. The brick outer face curls around and protects the courtyard. On the inner face, the façade is modulated in vertical strips of glass and white aluminium cladding, giving the impression that one can almost see under the skin of the building. The low-rise block and terraced housing are arranged in lines facing into gardens. Despite the traditional disguise of pitched roofs and chimneys, the disposition of openings, ramps and stairs brings a touch of surrealism to this part of the project, elevating it above the ordinary. In a Miróesque manner, the exciting architecture of Martínez-Lapeña and Torres is never quite what it seems.

Nearby, the block designed by Enrique Alvarez-Sala, Carlos Rubio Carvajal and César Ruíz-Larrea at Calle Viridiana 7/Calle de Mogambo 9 (1993), is a good example of the new housing type within the Madrid Sur development.

ADDRESS Colonia San José, Puerto del Milagro units 1–9, 28018 Madrid
CLIENT Instituto de la Vivienda de Madrid
AREA 39,554 square metres COST 1525 million pesetas
METRO *cercanía* to Entrevías (C1, C2) BUS 57, 144
ACCESS none

José Martínez-Lapeña and Elías Torres 1992–94

Vallecas

Vallecas

José Martínez-Lapeña and Elías Torres 1992–94

Mata del Agua Housing

Mark Fenwick and Javier Iribarren formed their practice in partnership with British architects Geoffrey Reid Associates in 1989, having previously worked with Junquera/Pérez-Pita. They received this commission as consolation for being runners-up in a EUROPAN housing competition.

The old village of Vallecas is cut off from other parts of Madrid by the M40 motorway and, despite the steady encroachment of housing and industry, has retained its own character. Reid Fenwick's development looks away from the town over agricultural land to the south of Madrid.

Each façade is different, giving the building identity and variety. At the top of the sloping site, a block of flats set behind framed access walkways looks down an internal street of terraced houses. Each of the houses is minimally composed with its own small terrace and first-floor balcony facing into the communal space. The units are stepped down the street, increasing their individual identity and making them appear like houses in a typical nineteenth-century British terrace. The combination of plants, people, washing and deep shadows animates the grey rendered façades. The central street gives focus to the community and is looked after with pride. The simple ingredients – identity, hierarchy and community – have been blended here to create a real sense of home.

ADDRESS Calle Mata del Agua 31 and Calle Umbrales 11, 28031 Madrid
CLIENT Empresa Municipal de la Vivienda
TECHNICAL ARCHITECT Lucinio Pérez
STRUCTURAL ENGINEER Alfonso Gómez Gaite
SIZE 30 houses and 11 apartments COST 190 million pesetas
METRO Miguel Hernández (line 1) then bus 142, or *cercanía* to Vallecas (C1, C2) then bus 142 BUS 142
ACCESS none

Reid Fenwick Asociados 1990–94

Reid Fenwick Asociados 1990–94

Centro

Madrid City Archive

As part of the agreement to redevelop the old Mahou brewery as private housing, the *Ayuntamiento* (city government) insisted that the oldest part of the building should be converted into a city archive. As a result, there is now an extraordinary contrast between the pink repro-hacienda architecture of the housing and Pérez Arroyo's well-mannered intervention.

The brick-clad, iron-framed brewery dates from the nineteenth century, though the roof was raised with a steel structure in the early twentieth century. The design conserves the existing fabric, adding obviously new elements where necessary. Entering from the street, one glimpses a courtyard, which is maintained as part of the development agreement. The archive's courtyard façade is clad in oxidised steel panels which bring to mind the rusted machinery found in the old brewery. Services run in the void between the oxidised steel panels and the brick inner skin. Original brickwork has been repointed, cleaned and left exposed.

A gallery encloses the courtyard and joins the housing to the archive. At first-floor level it contains a laboratory for document restoration. The x-shaped glazing bars were introduced as a modern counterpart to the original windows but take the intervention strategy a bit too far. At second-floor level a steel and glass pergola replaces a planted trellis, providing shelter for smokers banished from inside.

Internally, the existing iron structure has been treated and varnished. Where partitions have been added to provide office space, the solid panels stop 2.2 metres above floor level with glass above so that the clear span of the original structure remains visible.

The top floor is a reading room for researchers. The roof structure has been cut back along one side and tied with stainless steel rods, giving a double-height volume over the index cabinets, and preventing a clash between this new element and the old roof structure. Three levels of base-

Salvador Pérez Arroyo 1989–95

Salvador Pérez Arroyo 1989–95

ment have been created out of the original two beneath the courtyard. A robot was used to clear this area during demolition because of potential health hazards from alcohol fumes. The basements now contain more than 20 kilometres of mechanised shelving which has been designed with waterproof joints, so that the archives can be sealed from damage by sprinklers if there is a fire. Until recently, archives were usually protected by gas systems which starved fires of oxygen, but these are now considered environmentally unsound.

ADDRESS Calle Amaniel 29–31, 28015 Madrid
CLIENT Comunidad de Madrid
TECHNICAL ARCHITECTS Manuel Olave Parra and Fernando Olave García
AREA 4886 square metres COST 368 million pesetas
METRO San Bernando (lines 2, 4) BUS 147
ACCESS for genuine research projects only

Salvador Pérez Arroyo 1989–95

Salvador Pérez Arroyo 1989–95

Extension to the Senate

In the nineteenth century, the Augustine convent of Maria de Aragón was converted into chambers for the Senate. This extension provides a chamber and additional offices facing on to the busy Calle Bailen.

The semicircular council chamber at the front of the development is raised on a plinth. While the curve improves views of the elegant neighbouring Royal Belgian Mining Company building, the inaccessible plinth prevents the external spaces being brought into the public domain. The offices, which form a backdrop to the semi-cylinder, are focused around a five-storey atrium covered by a glazed barrel vault. A lower structure connects the offices and chamber to the old building and maintains the principal axis of the original Senate. The design is characterised by great eclecticism, with references to both Mario Botta and James Stirling, but it fails to achieve the geometric simplicity or sculptural impact of either of these masters.

Along the Calle del Rio the office building is cut back, though the overweight cornice carries on, supported on the corner of Calle del Reloj by an excessively tall and inelegant column. The open space between the office block and the original Senate appears redundant, the glazed wall at the end of the atrium facing into a dead zone.

The elevations are heavily handled and give an unapproachable air – hardly a desirable expression of the democratic and pro-European political regime now governing Spain.

ADDRESS Calle Bailen 5, 28013 Madrid
CLIENT Patrimonio del Senado
METRO Plaza España (lines 3, 10), Santo Domingo (line 2)
BUS 25, 33, 39, 148
ACCESS none

Centro

Salvador Gayarre Ruiz de la Galarreta 1988–92

Centro

Salvador Gayarre Ruiz de la Galarreta 1988–92

Casa de la Villa Car Park

City government officials from the *Ayuntamiento* used to park their cars on the plaza which originally sloped down to Calle de Sacramento. The new car park provides covered parking and access to offices as well as a public space in the heart of the old city.

The plaza has been raised to provide a flat surface with parking beneath. This creates a clear distinction between the public open space, the street and the car park entrances. (The depth of the car park was limited to protect archaeological remains of the old Arab quarter.) To provide the maximum number of spaces, parking is organised on a spiral ramp 15.5 metres wide: enough for two lanes of traffic with parking places either side. A central shaft, 5 metres in diameter, encloses air intake and extract ducts and other services. A secondary pedestrian ramp spirals around a full-height mushroom-headed column which supports the concrete waffle slab of the plaza above.

There are two vehicular entrances off Calle de Sacramento. These are situated on either side of a curved glass wall which allows natural light into the car park and exposes the blue steel trussed structure supporting the edge of the plaza behind. In front, a cascade fills the space between street level and car park level, the sound of water providing a delightful antidote to the city centre traffic. Away from the tourist trail, this is a tranquil and cool place to pause. The stepped granite scales of the waterfall catch the sunlight, casting sparkling reflections on to the glass wall. Unfortunately, the water has also left daubs of calcium deposit on the glass, reducing the transparency. At plaza level, a sand-blasted glass oculus lets light into an exhibition space below, a vestibule to underground entrances to offices in the Casa de Cisneros and Casa Consistorial. The granite-paved plaza itself lacks life – it needs seating, bins and lighting to encourage people to stop and spend time here.

Salvador Pérez Arroyo 1988–91

Pérez Arroyo's fascination with the application of technology is what gives his architecture distinctiveness in Spain. This thirst for invention was often let down in his early work by an inexperienced construction industry unable to realise his high-tech ambitions. Fortunately, the occasionally crude detailing of this project is resolved in later designs where architectural aspiration and constructional capability meet.

ADDRESS Calle de Sacramento (opposite number 5), 28005 Madrid
CLIENT Ayuntamiento de Madrid
TECHNICAL ARCHITECT Fernando Olave García
STRUCTURAL ENGINEERS J A Dominguez, J Izquierdo and J Ortiz
AREA 6500 square metres, 150 car parking spaces
COST 360 million pesetas
METRO La Latina (line 5) BUS 3, 31, 50, 65, 148
ACCESS to public square only

Salvador Pérez Arroyo 1988–91

Salvador Pérez Arroyo 1988–91

Plaza de Cascorro Housing

The oldest housing type in Madrid, the *corrala*, was arranged around a patio, with apartments reached by external galleries. Facing on to the street, its flat façades hid the density, colour and noise that lay behind.

This design by Mariano Bayón won several awards in 1987 for its subtle fusion of new brick housing with a nineteenth-century *corrala* block. The original yellow rendered building faces the Plaza de Cascorro at the heart of the Rastro market. It has been restored and its interiors have been replanned to give more efficient housing layouts. Beyond it, Bayón has designed a new block which follows the principles of *corrala* housing but exploits technology to achieve a modern expression.

Lightweight steel galleries and glazed canopies counterbalance the solid detailing of the original timber structure, while maintaining the same rhythm. The two blocks meet at the core, where glass balustrades articulate the junction and subtly join two architectural eras.

At ground level, retail units face into the courtyard, though they are shut off from the market and are now sadly empty. Beyond the granite-paved courtyard, a smaller lightwell forms a transition zone with views into the warren of alleys and interconnected patios beyond.

A similar restoration and intervention at Calle de Sombreria 16 (1995, Mateu, Lliso and Manzano) counterpoises two patios; one is modern, rendered and animated by steel balconies, the other is an original *corrala*.

ADDRESS Plaza de Cascorro 11, 28005 Madrid
CLIENT Empresa Municipal de la Vivienda
TECHNICAL ARCHITECT José Angel Azañedo
COST 120 million pesetas
METRO La Latina (line 5) BUS 17, 18, 23, 35, 60
ACCESS none

Mariano Bayón 1986–87

Centro

Mariano Bayón 1986–87

Centro

Embajadores Housing

The bulk of this project's street elevation is broken by deep vertical slots, small balconies and changes in angle of the brick façade. The overhanging steel cornice caps the building like the eaves of its older neighbours, while the rusticated brick and rubble-stone base provides a strong foundation along the steep slope of the street.

The organisation is based on the *corrala*, the internal courtyard plan typical of housing in the old quarters of central Madrid. A lightweight raised roof over the *corrala* allows light and air into the heart of the building; the central space also acts as a transition zone between street and apartments. At either end of the *corrala*, stairs and lifts lead to access balconies which are positioned 60 centimetres below the floor level of the flats so that there are no direct views into bedroom windows 1.8 metres above. Front doors, paired and set back, are reached via a small ramp. Courtyard walls are rendered and painted; glass blocks in the floor allow light into the car park below.

At every turn, the architects have striven to provide contextual architecture and a sense of community without resorting to historical mimicry.

ADDRESS Calle Embajadores 37, 28012 Madrid
CLIENT Empresa Municipal de la Vivienda
AREA 4100 square metres COST 205 million pesetas
METRO Lavapiés (line 3) BUS 27, 34, 36, 41, 60, 78, 116, 118, 119, 148
ACCESS none

Jesús San Vicente and Juan Mera 1989–90

Jesús San Vicente and Juan Mera 1989–90

Mercado de Anticuarios

Having won the limited competition to convert the central fish market into a design-orientated craft market, Domínguez and Peñalba joined forces with Aroca, drawing on his experience of construction and contract management. While other competitors had proposed managing the level change between the Puerta de Toledo and Plaza Campillo Mundo Nuevo by creating a transition zone in the centre of the building, the winners placed ramps and stairs adjacent to the plaza, leaving an atrium in the centre. The furniture shop bordering the Puerta de Toledo was the only new building in the project. Its rounded end faces on to the Glorieta and turns the corner on to the busy Ronda de Toledo.

Over many years of change, the layout of the old market building had become horrendously complex. Now, although the building remains a warren, extending the maze of streets of the neighbouring Rastro, a series of smaller voids grouped around the atrium make orientation easier.

In its first year, more than a million visitors passed through the market's doors, making it the most popular building in Madrid after the Prado. Now, of 140 shops only 31 are occupied and 500 jobs have been lost, the whole project a victim of bad management and poor publicity. Away from the entrance, long avenues of units lie deserted. A massive injection of energy and generous government incentive packages are urgently needed to prevent this building becoming an empty shell.

ADDRESS Ronda de Toledo 2, 28005 Madrid
CLIENT IMADE, Comunidad de Madrid
AREA 21,000 square metres COST 1000 million pesetas
METRO Puerta de Toledo (line 5) BUS 3, 17, 18, 23, 35, 41, 60, 148, C
ACCESS Tuesday to Saturday 10.30–21.00; Sunday 10.30–14.30

Martín Domínguez, Jesús Peñalba and Ricardo Aroca 1986–89

Martín Domínguez, Jesús Peñalba and Ricardo Aroca 1986–89

Puerta de Toledo

Juan Navarro Baldeweg has become one of Spain's best-known architects, developing an international portfolio and teaching at Princeton University. This makes it all the more curious that the collection of buildings to the north of the eighteenth-century Glorieta Puerta de Toledo represent the only commissions he has received in his home city. The buildings – a social services centre, a cultural centre, a kindergarten and a library – comprise part of a competition-winning masterplan to complete the area adjacent to the church of San Francisco el Grande. As part of the masterplan, commissions for new housing blocks along the Gran Via de San Francisco el Grande were handed out to a variety of well-known Madrileño architects, such as the Casas brothers and Jaime Lorenzo, Mariano Bayón and Salvador Pérez Arroyo, whose crinkly-tin housing scheme replaces an earlier project by Alejandro de la Sota.

The buildings designed by Baldeweg on both sides of the Calle de Toledo terminate the Gran Via and provide a new focus to the Glorieta. They are closely related, both in constructional technique and by their granite base, though they are each very distinct in form and context. The base conveys a sense of a gateway, providing a formal, tough entrance into the old part of the city. In baroque fashion, the grey granite walls splay out and the curving steps narrow to accentuate perspective.

Of the three buildings to the west, the cultural centre is dominant, with its curved triangular steel roof reducing scales between the Gran Via de San Francisco and the Glorieta. The arcaded entrance continues the line of columns set up by the neighbouring Ministry of Agriculture and Fisheries, although the rebate at roof level makes a conscious break in elevation as well as allowing clerestory light into the stairs. There is a constant play in Baldeweg's architecture, establishing relationships with neighbouring buildings and then breaking them down to assert individuality.

Juan Navarro Baldeweg 1985–87

Juan Navarro Baldeweg 1985–87

Set on top of the granite promontory, the social services and children's centres are more discreet. The curved brick façade of the kindergarten relates the project to its neighbours, drawing pedestrians into Calle de la Paloma. The Colmenar limestone-clad social services building is less dynamic but more muscular, providing a background to the smaller buildings in front and a gatehouse to the Calle de Toledo. At its feet, a two-storey gallery appears more whimsical, relating the coherent composition back to its fragmented context. The buildings' façades all appear austere – Baldeweg believes that the richness of a design comes through geometric and volumetric composition, rather than adornment.

Sadly, the interiors of all these buildings have been poorly maintained and are a shadow of the photographs published on their completion. Fortunately, Baldeweg's library opposite (see page 94) remains in much better condition.

ADDRESS Gran Via de San Franciscoel Grande 2 (cultural centre); Calle de la Paloma 39 (social services centre); Calle de la Paloma 23 (kindergarten) 28005 Madrid
CLIENT Comunidad de Madrid
STRUCTURAL ENGINEER Julio Martínez Calzón
AREA 1900 square metres (cultural centre); 1200 square metres (social services centre); 600 square metres (kindergarten)
METRO Puerta de Toledo (line 5) BUS 3, 17, 18, 23, 35, 41, 60, 148, C
ACCESS none to social services centre or kindergarten; cultural centre open Monday to Friday 9.00–21.30

Juan Navarro Baldeweg 1985–87

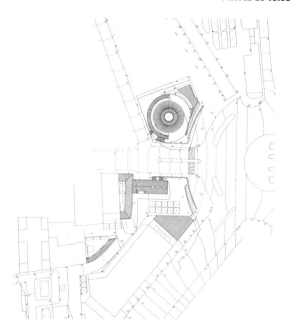

Juan Navarro Baldeweg 1985–87

Pedro Salinas Library

The cylindrical library sits on its own granite base on the Calle de Toledo, facing the three other buildings designed by Baldeweg (see page 90). Whereas across the road the granite promontory serves as a base for Baldeweg's cultural and social services centres and a termination to the Calle de Paloma, here it provides a plinth for the autonomous form of the library. In practical terms it acts as little more than a deserted terrace giving access to fire-escape stairs, the platform raised above pavements on all sides. The cylinder is clad in Colmenar limestone and acts as a powerful pivot between the Calle de Toledo and Mercado de Anticuarios (see page 88).

The spatially dynamic entrance is cut into the promontory. From here, top-lit stairs lead in three directions, drawing visitors into the main cylinder, cut back on this floor by a glass screen which gives views into an enclosed courtyard beyond. The screen allows light into the basement, where the children's library is housed.

Services are wrapped in a semicircle around the cylindrical body of the library. Curved stairs hug the external walls then arrive, disappointingly, next to the toilets. The reading rooms do not disappoint, however: the contextual games evident outside are here transferred to the inside. Volumetrically, the two floors are contained by the cylinder. In plan and section they subtly change from one side to another.

On the first floor, the section of the periodicals area is compressed, opening out over the book stacks. On the second floor, the reading room extends to the windows which look out over the Glorieta, while next to the book stacks it is cut back to form a mezzanine: a room within a room. The stacks themselves cascade back from the first-floor reading room, forming balustrades to narrow galleries. The ceiling of the first-floor reading space is lowered, emphasising the volume of the cylinder around.

Juan Navarro Baldeweg 1990–94

Juan Navarro Baldeweg 1990–94

Externally, the cylinder commands inevitable comparison to Asplund's Municipal Library in Stockholm. Internally, however, the simple volume of the Swedish masterpiece has been compromised by a welded oxidised steel baffle set beneath the central roof light. The critic William Curtis refers to 'spaces to stand under and understand' as a recurring theme in Baldeweg's designs. In this case the baffle lacks the compressive strength of the false ceiling to the floor below, and therefore reduces the spatial impact of this mezzanine level without achieving the focus of concentration or light for which it was conceived.

ADDRESS Glorieta Puerta de Toledo 1, 28005 Madrid
CLIENT Comunidad de Madrid
AREA 2450 square metres
METRO Puerta de Toledo (line 5)
BUS 17, 18, 23, 35, 41, 60, 148, C
ACCESS Monday to Friday 8.00–20.45; Saturday 9.00–13.45

Centro

Juan Navarro Baldeweg 1990–94

Juan Navarro Baldeweg 1990–94

San Francisco el Grande Housing 1

This project completes the swathe of new housing constructed between the Basilica of San Francisco el Grande and the Puerta de Toledo. The tautly curved ends, crinkly metal cladding and horizontal banding give the appearance of a giant liner moored at the entrance to the old heart of Madrid. At one stage in the design process Pérez Arroyo drew a sketch of the project complete with ship's funnels to emphasise this point.

The base and upper levels of the linear block step down two storeys towards the Puerta de Toledo in response to the sloping site. The ground level is predominantly glazed and will be occupied by retail units interspersed with the entrance lobbies to the flats above. These units stop short of the southern end to reveal a gymnastic concrete columnar support to the curved prow. A ramp connection to the public gardens behind skirts around this base.

The bands of glazing and golden cladding on the east façade emphasise horizontality, the mass softened by trees planted along the pavement in front. The gold colour of the cladding hints at the baroque origins of this part of the city. More importantly, it restricts glare from the building, permitting Pérez Arroyo simultaneously to persevere with an industrial aesthetic and to produce an architecture responsive to its urban setting.

ADDRESS Gran Via de San Francisco el Grande 5–9, 28005 Madrid
CLIENT Empresa Municipal de la Vivienda
METRO Puerta de Toledo (line 5) BUS 3, 17, 18, 23, 35, 41, 60, 148, C
ACCESS none

Salvador Pérez Arroyo 1995–96

Centro

Salvador Pérez Arroyo 1995–96

San Francisco el Grande Housing 2

The Basilica of San Francisco el Grande (designed by Francisco Sabatini in the eighteenth century) is one of the most easily recognisable buildings in Madrid. Bayón's housing block does little to interfere with its illustrious neighbour, presenting an unashamedly modern face to the street while making positive contextual gestures to the church. The splayed back corners are crowned by steel and glass towers, a modern interpretation of late nineteenth-century *torreones* or *miradores*. They also relate to the exuberant towers and cupolas next door.

The light-coloured limestone cladding from the Boñar quarry in Leon is carefully chosen to complement the church. Inlaid aluminium strips help to emphasise linearity and deflect water from the stone, preventing staining – a device Bayón learnt when he was conservation architect for the Congress building (restored 1983–86).

The interior courtyard contrasts with the street front. A steel frame applied to pale Alicante brick façades supports glass-fronted access balconies. There are clear similarities here with Bayón's earlier restoration and extension work on the Corrala de Cascorro (see page 84) with its typical old Madrid internal courtyard. The minimalist steel sculpture at the back of the patio is by the architect.

ADDRESS Gran Via de San Francisco el Grande 15–17, 28005 Madrid
CLIENT Empresa Municipal de la Vivienda
TECHNICAL ARCHITECT José Angel Azañedo
COST 206 million pesetas
METRO Puerta de Toledo (line 5) BUS 3, 17, 18, 23, 35, 41, 60, 148, C
ACCESS none

Mariano Bayón 1989–90

Centro

Mariano Bayón 1989–90

Retiro

Atocha Station

The original station (1888–92), a classic confection of iron and glass, was designed by Alberto del Palacio. In 1982, the Ministry of Public Works and Transport determined to overhaul the station, quadrupling its size to cope with increased rail traffic and provide metro and bus interchanges, car-rental facilities and parking. Around the same time, the *Ayuntamiento* planned the removal of a fly-over which crossed the Glorieta Carlos V, isolating the station. This 'Operation Atocha' took ten years to complete.

Moneo won a restricted competition for the redevelopment of Atocha in 1984. The principal problem was how to link the different levels of the site: the rail tracks and metro were variously positioned 8–17 metres below the bus station and surrounding roads. The brick cylinder provides the key component in resolving the circulation. Its strong form is visible from afar, shining out like a lantern signalling the entrance to the station. From here, escalators and stairs descend into the commuter (*cercanía*) concourse, the hub of Atocha.

The different components assume their own character at roof level. Over the *cercanía* tracks, shafts set between hemispherical aluminium canopies allow light into the concrete cavern below; an adjacent canopy sails over the long-distance trains. Rather than opt for a clear span envelope, Moneo has designed a roof closely related both to the geometry of the tracks and the axis of the original station, linking old and new structures. Ribbed oxidised steel umbrellas are separated by a grid of rooflights and supported on tall, slender concrete columns. Along the building's eastern side, a glazed curtain wall divides the local and long-distance platforms. The best view of this section is from the car park and drop-off zone, where a bridge divides the old and new sheds. Looking through the forest of columns, the sleek high-speed trains (AVES) present a thrilling picture as they wait to depart for Seville, bathed in shafts of sunlight.

Retiro

Rafael Moneo 1985–92

Rafael Moneo 1985–92

The old station is penetrated by travolators and stairs which link street level with the concourse, old with new. Trains have been completely removed, and del Palacio's elegant structure has been filled instead with a tropical garden. Steam jets create a humid atmosphere maintained at a constant 24 degrees centigrade. Cafés, information offices, ticket booths and waiting rooms line this tranquil respite from travel stress. The conversion of train shed to garden is an extraordinary civic gesture, introducing a dramatic internal space into the public domain.

Externally, an open plaza separates the new station entrance, old station structure and surrounding streets. The brick clock-tower dominates the space and provides a visual pivot to counterbalance the cylinder of the entrance building.

Successful on functional and architectonic levels, the station remains ironically isolated from the city by road traffic. Hostile six-lane roads cut it off from the Botanical Gardens, the Retiro and the Reina Sofía, while parking and buses dominate the street-level zones. The plaza in front of the station is subsequently deserted. Ripe with urban gestures, Atocha is still desperately in need of a visual and physical connection to the city it serves.

ADDRESS Glorieta de Atocha, 28012 Madrid
CLIENT Dirección General de Infraestructura del Transporte Ferroviario/ Ministerio de Obras Públicas y Transportes (MOPT)
COST 20,400 million pesetas
METRO Atocha RENFE (line 1), *cercanía* to Atocha (C1-8)
BUS 10, 14, 19, 24, 26, 32, 54, 57, 140, 141, C
ACCESS open

Rafael Moneo 1985–92

Rafael Moneo 1985–92

Centro de Arte Reina Sofía

The San Carlos Hospital was commissioned in the eighteenth century, on the initiative of Carlos III. The original design (1756–81, Francisco Sabatini) comprised a grand complex constructed around five internal courtyards. The fact that only one of these courtyards was ever built accounts for the austerity of the façades, only ever intended to face on to other patios. The initial conversion (1981–86) into a cultural centre was planned by Antonio Fernandez Alba. When José Guiro took over as director of the Reina Sofía, it was decided to transfer the permanent collection of the Museo Español de Arte Contemporaneo in the Ciudad Universitaria to the Reina Sofía. To facilitate the transformation into Spain's primary museum of modern art, Vázquez de Castro and Iñiquez de Onzoño were appointed to complete the conversion.

The most potent element of their masterplan is the addition of glass lift towers designed by the British team of Ian Ritchie and Ove Arup and Partners. Ritchie has been well known for technically sophisticated glass structures since his early work with Rice Francis Ritchie at La Villette in Paris. Here there are two public towers, each containing three lifts, which flank the entrance to the museum; a third, larger tower containing passenger lift, goods lift and escape stairs is on the north-west façade facing Calle del Hospital.

The skeletal primary steel structure of the towers is painted white. The glass enclosure affords maximum transparency so that the lifts can clearly be seen bobbing up and down between floors. Every part of the structure, every nut and bolt – even the cleaning gantry – is positively expressed as part of the architecture. Technology has been exploited to the point that it becomes decoration. The panes of glass are externally fixed by bolted stainless steel arms to paired, tensed stainless steel cables. Movement in the glass is accommodated by the rotational action of the sleeved bolts

Retiro

Antonio Vázquez de Castro, José Luis Iñiguez de Onzoño 1988–90

Antonio Vázquez de Castro, José Luis Iñiguez de Onzoño 1988–90

and the vertical movement of giant springs (to which the cables are fixed) anchored to the ground. The glass is internally fixed back to the steel structure by slotted steel brackets. The slots permitted tolerance during construction and now enable lateral movement of each pane under wind load.

The interior of the museum is subdued by comparison, having been subtly transformed with respect for the original architecture. Galleries fill the old hospital wards and surround a cool, peaceful courtyard watched over by Alexander Calder's kinetic sculpture *Carmen* (1974). White walls, marble floors, vaulted ceilings and controlled daylighting are entirely complementary to the exhibition of art. Along the shorter sides of the courtyard the arcaded galleries have been glazed, providing a climatically controlled transitional space between the outside world and the exhibits. The permanent collection housed on Level 2 includes Picasso's renowned civil war masterpiece *Guernica* (1937).

Although the Reina Sofía is currently the most important modern art museum in Spain, it will be interesting to see if it can retain this position in the face of inevitable competition from Barcelona's Museo d'Arte Contemporani (Richard Meier and Partners, 1995).

ADDRESS Calle Santa Isabel 52, 28012 Madrid
CLIENT Ministerio de Cultura
TECHNICAL ARCHITECT Antonio Palomo Herranz
GLASS LIFT DESIGN Ian Ritchie Architects and Ove Arup and Partners
AREA 55,000 square metres COST 4500 million pesetas
METRO Atocha (line 1) BUS 6, 26, 32, 57, 59, 85, 86
ACCESS Monday, Wednesday to Saturday 10.00–21.00;
Sunday 10.00–14.30

Retiro

Antonio Vázquez de Castro, José Luis Iñiguez de Onzoño 1988–90

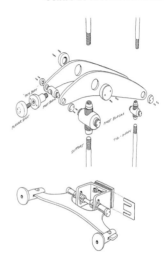

Antonio Vázquez de Castro, José Luis Iñiguez de Onzoño 1988–90

Auditorium, Centro de Arte Reina Sofía

The auditorium – one of a number of interventions introduced at the Centro de Arte Reina Sofía (see page 108) – is a testament to the skill of the renowned Catalan architects Jaume Bach and Gabriel Mora.

Situated on the ground floor in a former hospital ward, the layout is determined by the original configuration: the space is divided into two unequal portions by a 2-metre-thick wall punctured by an arch and two square side openings. Both spaces are little more than 7 metres wide, with barrel-vaulted ceilings. Bach and Mora's approach respects the original form of the spaces while introducing a series of new elements independent of the existing structure. The smaller of the two spaces now forms an anteroom to the lecture theatre. A triangular projection booth is positioned beyond the punctured dividing wall, subdividing circulation into the two side aisles and offering a visual contrast to the stone-dressed arch.

The floor of the theatre has been raked to improve sightlines and hide services. Finishes have been selected to improve acoustic performance: for example, the grey-painted triangular panel suspended over the dais helps to deflect sound down to the audience. It also relates to the shape of the projection box, continuing an architectural theme where functional elements are visually linked to each other and consciously separated from the existing structure.

ADDRESS Calle Santa Isabel 52, 28012 Madrid
CLIENT Ministerio de Cultura
STRUCTURAL ENGINEERS Brufau, Obiol, Moya y Asociados SA
SERVICES AND ACOUSTICS ENGINEER Gerado García-Ventosa
AREA 266 square metres COST 100 million pesetas
METRO Atocha (line 1) BUS 6, 26, 32, 57, 59, 85, 86
ACCESS for events

Retiro

Jaume Bach and Gabriel Mora 1986–87

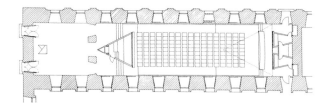

Jaume Bach and Gabriel Mora 1986–87

Exhibition Greenhouse, Real Jardín Botánico de Madrid

Containing more than 1200 plant species, the exhibition greenhouse replaces the 1929 structure demolished in 1975. Its design represents a successful collaboration between architect, botanists, gardeners, energy consultants and engineers.

Angel Fernandez-Alba trained in the US and the UK, where he developed interests in the latest building technology. During the design of this project he returned to Britain to study technical solutions to the brief, and many of the components come from there, including the lacquered aluminium roof profiles, the perforated blinds and the glass.

The greenhouse forms part of the boundary to the gardens. The linear building is orientated east–west for maximum solar radiation, and divided into four sections. Potting and gardeners' areas are in the obscure glazed end, its reduced scale and curved form creating an entrance into the three distinct climatic zones of desert, sub-tropical and tropical. Mechanical plant is placed in basements at either end of the greenhouse.

The exploitation of passive energy sources largely determines the architectural expression. Double-glazing allows infra-red rays to penetrate the zones but reflects harmful ultraviolet rays. Solar energy is trapped in the glass cavity, keeping the temperature inside higher than outside. On the upper level, 160 square metres of solar panels intercept solar radiation. In summer this energy is stored below ground, to be released in winter. Energy is also harnessed from the water-table, 25 metres deep, where temperatures constantly range between 13 and 15 degrees centigrade. In summer this helps to cool the greenhouse, and in winter to heat it.

Temperatures are controlled in three ways. A system of louvres prevents excess solar radiation. If temperatures continue to rise, steam sprinklers are activated in the tropical section. They force evaporation,

Retiro

Angel Fernandez-Alba 1990–93

Angel Fernandez-Alba 1990–93

the steam absorbing heat to create vapour and reduce temperatures. If this fails, heat pumps transfer cold air stored in the water-table through steel grilles set in the floor. In this way, maximum temperatures are maintained at 30–35 degrees centigrade in the desert zone, 30–32 degrees in the sub-tropical zone, and 28–30 degrees in the tropical zone. A computer monitors the environment every ten seconds.

The architecture achieves great rigour through the clear expression of applied technology: the castellated steel portal frame is tied by tension wires and fixed to concrete bases; an aluminium cleaning gantry runs along the pitched roof on stainless steel tubular rails. A steel mesh walkway gives views down into the three zones.

ADDRESS Plaza de Murillo 2, 28014 Madrid
CLIENT Real Jardín Botánico de Madrid, Consejo Superior de Investigaciones Cientificas
STRUCTURAL ENGINEER Alfonso Gómez Gaite and Jesús Jiménez Cañas
CLIMATOLOGIST Manuel Fernandez
AREA 700 square metres
METRO Atocha (line 1)
BUS 10, 14, 19, 24, 26, 27, 32, 34, 45, 54, 57, 140, C
ACCESS 10.00–21.00 (summer), 10.00–18.00 (winter)

Angel Fernandez-Alba 1990–93

Retiro

Retiro

Angel Fernandez-Alba 1990–93

Consejo Economico y Social

Next to the Consejo (Council for Social and Economic Affairs) is a 1940s building, now a government ministry, which originally housed the Casa Sindical. Designed by Francisco Cabrero and Rafael Aburto, its gridded façade was inspired by Italian fascist design, but it has since been re-evaluated as a triumph of Spanish rationalism. The building which now contains the Consejo was also designed by Cabrero and Aburto, and in the same style. It was built in 1959 to house the offices and printing works of the Falangist newspaper *Pueblo*. With the advent of democracy the newspaper folded and the building acquired its current role: an arbitration centre for the state and unions.

The original steel structure supports the office tower which used to span the *Pueblo* printing works below. The redevelopment took the separated functions of the original building as the basis for the revamp: meeting rooms and conference halls are located on the lower levels with offices in the tower. The old lightwell to the printing floors has been enclosed by a glass-block cylinder which bursts out from the building at certain points, allowing a diffuse light to penetrate public areas. Flanking walls to the atrium are cut with circular openings framing steel bridges.

The exterior of the tower has been cleaned and new glazing installed, abstracting the original grid of mullions and transoms. The oxidised steel sculpture on the entrance façade is by José Luis Sanchez. It hides the words *Diario Pueblo* inscribed in the granite.

ADDRESS Calle de las Huertas 71, 28014 Madrid
CLIENT Ministerio de Trabajo y Securidad Social
AREA 14,900 square metres COST 1900 million pesetas
METRO Antón Martín (line 1) BUS 10, 14, 27, 34, 37, 45
ACCESS entrance area only

José Antonio Galea 1990–93

Retiro

José Antonio Galea 1990–93

Galería A+A

A subsidiary of the Obalne Gallery in Piran, this is the only gallery outside Slovenia dedicated to the exhibition of work by Slovenian artists. In homage to its location, however, once a year the gallery is used for an exhibition of work by a Madrileño artist. It was located in Madrid as part of the city's celebrations as 1992 European Capital of Culture. Although he now practises in Vienna, Boris Podrecca originally came from Slovenia and he was therefore a natural choice to design these two exquisite spaces. The project shows off both the constructive approach typical of current Viennese architecture and Podrecca's own Mediterranean origins.

The two galleries are situated on either side of an entrance hall which leads to apartments above. The asymmetrically positioned iron column common to both spaces is an original feature, and it is the starting point for the whole design: Podrecca uses the asymmetry to link the two rooms and to create a symmetrical organisation, with one gallery mirroring the other. Steel, clear-glass and etched-glass entrance screens emphasise this symmetry.

Spot lighting is fixed to two electrified steel tracks which cantilever off the iron column. Lights can be positioned anywhere along these tracks to suit particular exhibits. Suspended ceilings are pulled back from walls and appear to float. The floors are finished with a dark grey Slovenian limestone rebated at the edges in a visual reference to islands off the coast near Piran.

Differentiation of spaces is achieved by the sycamore-veneered MDF furniture. The sycamore has been carefully laid to create a chequered pattern to the vertical surfaces. In one gallery, a multifunctional pod contains a toilet, cupboard and fold-down desk. Steps leading to a storage area are extended to become bookshelving. Extraordinarily economic in its use of space, the pod is also exquisitely detailed, with clear expression

Retiro

Boris Podrecca 1992

Retiro

Boris Podrecca 1992

of veneered planes and structural steelwork. In the adjacent gallery, a veneered door forms the end wall. It can be rolled open on a timber wheel to reveal more storage space for works of art.

The combination of simple spaces offset by sensually detailed interventions turns the gallery itself into a work of art. Podrecca's skill has ensured that far from dominating the works on display, the architecture complements them, so that the art becomes the true protagonist of the space.

ADDRESS Calle San Pedro 9, 28014 Madrid
CLIENT Obalne Galerije
EXECUTIVE ARCHITECT Martín Domínguez
AREA 36 square metres
COST 100,000 Deutschmarks
METRO Atocha (line 1) BUS 6, 26, 32, 57
ACCESS Monday to Friday 17.00–21.00;
Saturday 12.00–14.00,
17.00–21.00

Retiro

Boris Podrecca 1992

Retiro

Boris Podrecca 1992

Museo Thyssen-Bornemisza

The Villahermosa Palace was built by Alessandro Pico della Mirandola in the late eighteenth century. In 1771, ownership passed to the Duke of Villahermosa who commissioned López Aguado to reconfigure the plan. His work began a series of interventions which have continually changed the internal layout of the building, but which have left the original exterior relatively unscathed. In 1973, the López-Quesada Bank acquired the building, once more cleared out the interior, excavated three basements and moved the main entrance back on to Calle Zorilla. By 1980, the López-Quesada Bank had collapsed, and the palace had been bought by the Bank of Spain and left to lie in a state of splendid decay.

During the 1980s, bids were submitted by a number of cities to receive, on loan, the extraordinary art collection of Baron Hans-Heinrich Thyssen-Bornemisza. Begun by the baron's father in the 1920s, the collection numbered nearly 800 paintings ranging from medieval pieces to works from the present day, and could no longer be displayed as a whole in the baron's Villa Favorita in Lugano, Switzerland. Various reasons are cited for Madrid's selection as home for the collection, but the most important factor was the offer of a redeveloped Palacio de Villahermosa. It now completes the city's 'golden triangle' of art museums, along with the Centro de Arte Reina Sofía and the Museo del Prado, and is one of the highlights of any visit to Madrid.

The building has been magnificently restored, extended and reorganised. Moneo's strategy was to work with the original architectural principles of the palace. The entrance has once again been positioned through the north façade off a tranquil private garden, creating a north–south axis around which the museum is organised. The volumes of the entrance hall and bookshop are compressed, with light filling the covered toplit patio beyond. The patio is the heart of the museum, around which visitors circu-

Rafael Moneo 1989–92

Rafael Moneo 1989–92

late. Indirect rooflights give a constant light plane on the Colmenar lime-stone floor and pink-wash walls. This combination of finishes is repeated in the galleries, absorbing light and giving spaces great serenity.

The journey around the museum begins with medieval works on the second floor, from where it is possible to look out over the patio rooflights and catch glimpses of the brick façades of offices above. Along the east wing, the chequered marble floor of the Villahermosa gallery leads into a series of perpendicular galleries displaying sixteenth-century Italian, German and Dutch paintings. Daylight is filtered by sculptural rooflights placed above each gallery. Louvres are controlled by photo-electric cells, ensuring that works are always exhibited under the same light levels. The west galleries are smaller, compressed spaces, open to the circulation route like a series of caves along a seashore.

Progressing through the museum, one sees slight differences between the galleries, though the consistent finishes and exemplary servicing (designed by Ove Arup and Partners) create a homogenous atmosphere. The view along the western galleries to the secondary stair offers an almost celestial experience. In Moneo's work, minimalism has come to represent not so much an expression of modernity, but rather a deep-rooted respect for traditional Spanish architectural values.

ADDRESS Palacio de Villahermosa, Paseo del Prado 8, 28014 Madrid
CLIENT Thyssen-Bornemisza Foundation
STRUCTURAL AND SERVICES ENGINEERS Ove Arup and Partners
AREA 18,000 square metres COST 4000 million pesetas
METRO Banco de España (line 2) BUS 9, 10, 14, 27, 34, 37, 45
ACCESS Tuesday to Saturday 10.00–19.00

Retiro

Rafael Moneo 1989–92

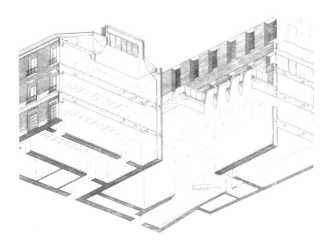

Rafael Moneo 1989–92

Offices for the Congress of Deputies

The young Catalan architects Clos, Rubert de Ventos and Parcerisa were selected ahead of 105 other entrants in a national competition to design this extension to the Spanish parliament. The original building (1843–50) was designed by Narciso Pascual y Colomer, and houses the debating chambers. The new extension contains offices for MPs and staff, meeting rooms and ancillary services.

The split organisation is uninspiring. The lower section mimics rather than abstracts its neo-classical parent. Above, a sinuous black glass façade takes the form of a knife, curving back at its east end so as not to dominate the Palacio del Congreso. The two disparate treatments have little to do with each other, and the forbidding dark glass of the façade seems to contradict the principles of democracy.

The entrance, through a glazed slot in the west elevation, promises some volumetric dynamism but immediately disappoints, leading to a pokey single-volume lobby.

For such a critically important expression of national optimism, this building is sadly impotent. Spanish architects have reinvented the public realm in recent years with vanguardist designs consistently among the best in Europe. But here the opportunity to construct a piece of architecture representative of the new Spain has been lost.

ADDRESS Calle de Zorrilla, 28014 Madrid
METRO Sevilla, Banco de España (line 2)
BUS 9, 10, 14, 27, 34, 37, 45
ACCESS none

Clos, Rubert de Ventos and Parcerisa 1986–90

Retiro

Clos, Rubert de Ventos and Parcerisa 1986–90

RENFE Offices

RENFE, the state railway company, underwent a total image change in 1992 with the introduction of high-speed trains and the redevelopment of Madrid's Atocha Station (see page 104) and Santa Justa in Seville. This prototype ticket and information office by Enrique Alvarez-Sala, Carlos Rubio Carvajal and César Ruíz-Larrea is entirely in keeping with the change.

Full-height glazing set in the existing façade gives clear views into the interior. A glass canopy cantilevers out over the pavement to signal the way in. The ground floor has been cut back to enable the whole triple-height space to be perceived as one. A mezzanine level of offices compresses the section over the ground-floor desks. These offices are enclosed by a translucent glass and steel screen stopped just beneath a suspended barrel-vaulted sycamore-veneered ceiling.

Walnut-finished stairs lead down to the basement level. Inlets cut into the grey granite walls provide booths for pay phones and help to illuminate the space via pavement lights above – not entirely necessary, since the basement is already flooded with light from ground-floor glazing.

The combination of so many different materials and colours appears excessive. Nevertheless, the creation of space and the introduction of light is extremely well handled, compensating for the over-exuberant detailing.

The murals by the entrance and the colour treatment of stairs and walls are by the Madrileño artist Carlos Pascual de Lara.

ADDRESS Calle Alcalá 44, 28014 Madrid
CLIENT Red Nacional de Ferrocarriles Españoles (RENFE)
AREA 1500 square metres COST 125 million pesetas
METRO Banco de España (line 2) BUS 5, 15, 20, 51, 52, 53, 150
ACCESS Monday to Friday 9.30–22.00

Alvarez-Sala, Rubio Carvajal and Ruíz-Larrea 1992

Retiro

Alvarez-Sala, Rubio Carvajal and Ruíz-Larrea 1992

Bar del Diego

Fernando del Diego opened his own cocktail bar having achieved legendary status as the barman at Chicote, the 1930s bar on Gran Via designed by Guiterrez Soto.

The design of Bar del Diego fuses a traditional ambience with modern aspiration without resorting to the transient gimmickry found in many similar establishments in Barcelona. The original façade has been retained, though the automatic glass door is new. The bar itself, which is raised half a storey above street level, is reached by a marble stair. A sloped glass box in the entrance hall encloses timber stairs which descend to the toilets, previously part of a neighbouring building. The glass box breaks up the entrance space, making it feel informal, though the transparency of the enclosure maintains a sense of spaciousness.

The hall is separated from the bar by a glass screen suspended from the original structure on steel cables. Alongside the stair it becomes a display cabinet for rare liqueurs, supported on a stainless steel tubular frame. Timber, leather, brass and mirrors create a timeless, welcoming atmosphere, while the precision of the glazed screen, the slimness of the suspended glass entrance canopy and the elegant stainless steel and ash lamps root the design in the present. The use of timber for walls, floors and furniture creates warmth, all the better for enjoying Señor del Diego's subtle concoctions. To appreciate the design fully, it is best to arrive early, leave late and have at least two of the house speciality, a 'Diego'.

ADDRESS Calle de la Reina 12, 28004 Madrid
CLIENT Fernando del Diego
AREA 100 square metres COST 15 million pesetas
METRO Gran Via (lines 1, 5) BUS 1, 2, 3, 40, 46, 74, 146, 149
ACCESS 18.00–3.00 daily

Retiro

Javier Maroto and Alvaro Soto 1992

Retiro

Javier Maroto and Alvaro Soto 1992

Salamanca and Chamberi

Cultural Centre for the Circulo de Lectores

Enric Miralles stands at the forefront of the modern European avant-garde. His work manipulates the inherent plasticity of architecture to obtain fluidity of space. In this pursuit, every component of any project he undertakes has a role to play and an identity of its own. The immediately chaotic, almost deconstructivist, appearance of his architecture soon reveals itself as the exact opposite: highly organised and celebrating the craftsmanship of building.

This project transformed a ground-floor retail unit in a dull 1950s block into the cultural foundation of the Circulo de Lectores. The space is used for the presentation of new authors and titles, conferences, readings, lectures and meetings. From the start, Miralles' aim was to create 'a single space which changes for each event, where informal conversation can take place in every corner'. The intervention works with the inherited plan form to achieve this goal.

Offices are lifted up to form mezzanines, compressing the volumes of the entrance area and meeting rooms. The curved form of these balconies seems to be kept from bursting by the sturdy, tubular steel ring beam suspended on steel rods from the ceiling.

Birch-laminated suspended ceilings hide services, dipping and weaving through the space to guide one gently into the main hall. Floor finishes change from brown marble to carpet, working with every other part of the architecture to create an organic rationale.

The concrete columns of the original structure have been enclosed in an aerodynamic casing of birch-ply and steel. Video screens set into the casing relay images from the main lecture hall. Miralles describes these column casings as being 'like fish, sliding between the public'. He has succeeded in transforming a rigid and rather inconvenient remnant of the

original building into a proactive element of the new architecture.

The design of the auditorium is filled with marine analogies. The language of white walls, ply, white steel and spindly secondary metalwork established in the entrance is compounded here by clearer boating forms. At mezzanine level, the glazed projection room, appearing like a control tower, is reached by a gangplank. The seating gallery is protected by a timber and steel tongue resembling a ship's prow. The balustrades and stair treads, painstakingly detailed, hang down from mezzanine galleries mimicking the access stairs of a liner. Even the services hum like a ferry.

Every part of the interior has been carefully thought out, from chairs to toilets to dais. Miralles is a great admirer of Gaudí's contemporary, Josep Jujol, and the dexterity with which he mixes spatial manipulation and detail resolution confirms him as the rightful inheritor of the *modernista* mantle.

ADDRESS Calle O'Donnell 10, 28009 Madrid
CLIENT Circulo de Lectores
STRUCTURAL ENGINEER Areinsa
SERVICES ENGINEERS Albert Salazar and Joan Carlos Navarro
AREA 1000 square metres COST 80 million pesetas
METRO Principe de Vergara (lines 2, 9) BUS 2, 28
ACCESS by appointment only, Monday to Friday 9.00–14.00 and 15.00–18.00 (telephone 435 36 14)

Enric Miralles 1991–92

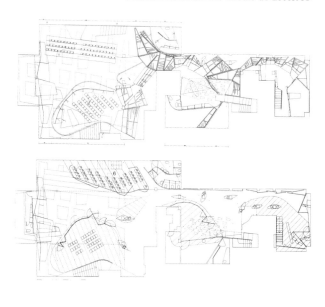

Enric Miralles 1991–92

California Café

The California chain of shops was refurbished to compete with VIPS and BOBS stores. The design of this two-storeys-and-a-basement mix of restaurants, cafés, bars, delicatessen, cake shop and newsagent shows similarities to other Allende-designed shop interiors, though the angled glass façade is on a larger scale than his Librería Crisol (1989, Calle Goya 18) and the stair design is more elaborate than at Don Algodon (1989, Calle Claudio Coello 58).

The design is full of nautical references. The marine-like balustrades are made of thin stainless steel tubes and tensioned wires, while the first-floor bar mimics the prow of a boat. The external steel escape stair hoisted up over the entrance would look quite at home fixed to the side of a ferry.

Angled suspended ceilings painted red or black help to suppress the section over the first-floor perimeter café seating; they also emphasise the linearity of the ground-floor bar. A line of thin columns divides the spaces visually and functionally. The 'Dry Martini' bar stools were especially designed by Pedro Miralles.

Although many of the details lack sophistication, the overall composition, white-jacketed waiters and marine typology mark California out as an exciting interior in a city dominated by conservative cafés and traditional shops.

ADDRESS Calle Goya 47, 28001 Madrid
CLIENT Diacal SA
AREA 1500 square metres COST 96 million pesetas
METRO Velázquez (line 4) BUS 21, 53
ACCESS Monday to Thursday, Sunday 7.30–22.45;
Friday, Saturday 7.30–23.45

Salamanca and Chamberi

Gabriel Allende 1989

Salamanca and Chamberi

Gabriel Allende 1989

Ekseption

Eduardo Samsó made his name designing fashionable bars in Barcelona. His skills were brought to Madrid by Bernard Beteinberg and Pepe Barroso for the crafting of three shop interiors, including this one.

The rounded steel canopy protruding from the existing granite façade offers a clue to the fairytale interior. The entrance bridge is an abstraction of a catwalk, lit by stainless steel bollard-lighting and animated by a series of video screens.

The main space oozes invention. The existing structure has been encased in steel, mimicking a car or plane prototype. Original ceilings are blue, suspended ceilings white. At the back of the shop the ceiling curves out of view beyond the changing rooms, as if wrapping up the shop. The gentle curve of the changing rooms – each one behind an acid-etched door – also seems to enclose the shop floor.

Rough and smooth elements are constantly placed next to each other, the contrasts in texture emphasising the silky refinement of the merchandise. Staff, clothes, shoes and shop defy the normally stuffy, traditional appearance of most Madrileño retail outlets. This is a world where nightclub and fashion seem to merge.

Samsó's other stores maintain the same levels of invention but offer a complete contrast. A minimalist Ekseption (1992, Avenida Concha Espina 14, 28036 Madrid) is dominated by stage lighting, while the Stephane Kelian shoe shop (1994, Calle Serrano 98, 28006 Madrid) displays great ingenuity to make the most out of a minute space.

ADDRESS Calle Velázquez 28, 28001 Madrid
CLIENT Bernard Beteinberg and Pepe Barroso
METRO Velázquez (line 4) BUS 1, 9, 19, 51, 74
ACCESS Monday to Saturday 10.30–14.30, 17.00–21.00

Eduardo Samsó 1989–90

Angela Navarro Beauty Centre

The beauty centre is at the end of a pedestrianised alley, on the top two floors of a 1910 building in one of the most affluent parts of Salamanca.

The façade has been conserved, but the interior has been completely redesigned. It features elements that recur in the work of Solans, Briales and del Amo: the fragmentation of space within a single volume and the clear functional expression of constructional components. Elaborate paired steel beams fixed to steel columns support the opaque and clear glazed roof. The structure gives rhythm and order to the beauty centre, so that the rooms, on two floors, can adopt a more abstract arrangement to suit functions. On the lower level, the rear space is taken up by staff areas with the main salon to the street side. Up the folded steel-plate stairs, the mezzanine floor is cut back to create a variety of double-height spaces. The treatment rooms, stores and modelling cubicles are enclosed by varnished MDF partitions incised with diamond-shaped windows looking down to the lower level. Partitions are only 2.1 metres high, leaving the roof plane to protect the centre like an umbrella.

While the definition of the different parts of the centre is clearly handled, at every point there is reference to the whole volume. Staff and clients can feel in harmony as they go in search of the body beautiful.

ADDRESS Callejón de Jorge Juan 12, 28001 Madrid
CLIENT Angela Navarro
COST 30 million pesetas
METRO Serrano, Velázquez (line 4) BUS 1, 9, 19, 51, 74
ACCESS treatment appointments Monday to Saturday 10.30–18.00
(telephone 431 11 80)

José Luis Solans, Pilar Briales and Ricardo del Amo 1990

Salamanca and Chamberí

José Luis Solans, Pilar Briales and Ricardo del Amo 1990

National Library

Founded in 1712, the National Library moved into its present building, designed by an engineer, Antonio Ruíz de Salces, in 1892. Four internal courtyards were surrounded by a three-storey circulation ring and divided by a cross of accommodation. At the centre of the cross was the reading room.

Low-quality modifications took their toll. A third of the building along Calle Serrano was subsequently used to house the Archaeology Museum, destroying the circulation ring. A labyrinth of corridors, secondary stairs and mezzanines was introduced to service increasingly autonomous departments, and one of the courtyards was filled in.

Begun in 1987, Junquera/Pérez-Pita's phased redevelopment has rejuvenated the library with a series of subtle, contextual and modern interventions. Initially, independent entities such as the National Book Service and the newspaper archive were moved to other premises, freeing space and allowing a rationalisation of the building's organisation. Four separate zones were then identified for public reading, research, public spaces (museum, exhibition, bookshop) and administration.

Having defined these areas, the architects set about streamlining the circulation through the building by inserting cores into the two main courtyards. All the elements of the library are related to these cores by lateral routes which, in effect, re-establish the ring of circulation cut by the Archaeology Museum. The curved cores are unmistakably modern, clad in a smooth, taut skin of Colmenar limestone rebated from the original courtyard façades. Internally, this definition is reinforced by pulling new elements away from the nineteenth-century elevations, leaving a double-height volume and contrasting the new palette of white walls, oiled oak floors and stainless steel with the original stone and brick.

The architects have endeavoured to restore principal spaces wherever

Jerónimo Junquera and Estanislao Pérez-Pita 1989, 1993, 1995

Jerónimo Junquera and Estanislao Pérez-Pita 1989, 1993, 1995

possible, but where new elements are needed they have drawn on original dimensions, scale and austerity to create a thoroughly modern counterpoint to the old. This is particularly apparent in the administrative wing, placed above the building perpendicular to the east–west axis and reached by separate lifts and stairs off the main entrance halls. Linear open-plan offices are separated from original façades by glass floors and voids. The glass and steel elevations on to the central patio clearly identify the origins of the extension but also abstract the rhythm of the original patio façade.

Service co-ordination and detailing are exemplary throughout, showing that modernism and craftsmanship are not mutually exclusive. Pérez-Pita cites 'place' as the starting point for all the practice's architecture. Here, they have used the architect's traditional tools – structure, light, technology, space, materials – to make a successful new building out of a Gordian knot.

ADDRESS Paseo de Recoletos 22, 28001 Madrid
CLIENT Ministerio de Cultura, Organismo Autonomo Biblioteca Nacional
STRUCTURAL ENGINEER Alfonso Gómez Gaite
SERVICES ENGINEER CIASA
AREA 35,800 square metres COST 2800 million pesetas
METRO Serrano (line 4), *cercanía* to Recoletos (C1, 2, 7, 8)
BUS 5, 14, 27, 37, 45, 53, 150
ACCESS Library: Monday to Friday 9.00–21.00; Saturday 9.00–14.00. Exhibitions: Tuesday to Saturday 10.00–21.00; Sunday 10.00–14.00. Bookshop: Monday 16.00–20.00; Tuesday to Friday 10.00–14.00, 15.00–20.00; Saturday 10.00–14.00

Jerónimo Junquera and Estanislao Pérez-Pita 1989, 1993, 1995

Jerónimo Junquera and Estanislao Pérez-Pita 1989, 1993, 1995

Cultural Institute, French Embassy

López-Riobóo and Sanz were commissioned to design the French Embassy's cultural centre after an open competition between French and Spanish architects. The building's symmetrical façade symbolises authority, and reflects the change in level between Calle Marqués de la Ensenada and the raised Plaza de la Villa de Paris. Two walls of granite form a plinth to the building and define the entrance, while an oxidised-steel and glass curtain wall encloses the offices above. The curtain wall is double-glazed, with the front face open to allow air circulation between the skins. The façade is capped by an oxidised-steel canopy which terminates the building and frames the different planes of the elevation.

A curved brick screen creates a hierarchy between the public entrance to the institute and the more private entrance to embassy offices. The entrance zone is compressed by the loggia of the bookshop above, with the light-filled double height of the reception hall beyond. The ground floor is succinctly organised, with architectural devices used to signpost different areas. A wide stair leads down to the lecture hall, and a smaller staircase links the bookshop and adjacent French Lycée. The glazed wall at the end of the hall creates a transition to the tranquil courtyard beyond.

ADDRESS Calle Marqués de la Ensenada 10, 28004 Madrid
CLIENT French Ministry of Foreign Affairs
TECHNICAL ARCHITECTS Eduardo Maldonado and Fernando García
STRUCTURAL ENGINEER ETESA
SERVICES ENGINEER CIASA
AREA 9000 square metres COST 1000 million pesetas
METRO Colón (line 4), *cercanía* to Recoletos (C1, 2, 7, 8)
BUS 5, 14, 21, 27, 45, 53, 150
ACCESS Cultural Institute open Monday to Friday 8.00–22.00

Juan López-Riobóo and José Manuel Sanz 1992–94

Salamanca and Chamberi

Juan López-Riobóo and José Manuel Sanz 1992–94

Alcalá Galiano Offices

These offices are in a once residential district which has now been taken over by government buildings, embassies and offices.

The city council insisted that three floors of parking should be provided if the existing building was to be extended to provide additional office space in the rear courtyard. The elegant minimalist architecture is a direct response to this planning requirement.

Due to the compactness of the site, intermediary columns would have reduced flexibility and restricted parking. The floor slabs therefore span from front to back. The whole front façade acts as a Vierendeel beam, transferring load to the side walls. The structure determined the 3 x 3 metre steel channel grid of the glazed façade. Upper levels appear to float above the glazed ground floor. Side walls are finished in concrete, but the rear wall is timber veneered. A steel and glass stair runs up this wall, maintaining the transparent theme.

As soon as the offices were occupied, an invasion of computer wires and Post-It notes inevitably followed, but the impact of the orthogonal façade remains strong. The delight of such architectural purity is emphasised by comparison with the looming bulk of the Heron Towers behind. These were originally designed, and recently extended, by Estudio Lamela (1967, 1989).

ADDRESS Calle Alcalá Galiano 4, 28010 Madrid
CLIENT Metaltrade SA
TECHNICAL ARCHITECT Vicente Arenas
AREA 1100 square metres COST 100 million pesetas
METRO Colón (line 4) BUS 5, 14, 21, 27, 45, 150
ACCESS none

Alvarez-Sala, Rubio Carvajal and Ruíz-Larrea 1990–91

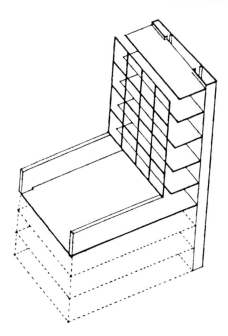

Alvarez-Sala, Rubio Carvajal and Ruíz-Larrea 1990–91

Marlborough Art Gallery

From the outside, this Franco-era building is dull and ill-suited to the salubrious Calle Orfila. Past the stainless steel and glass doors, however, Gluckman has created a serene, light-filled space. This is the Madrid branch of the internationally renowned gallery; others are in London, New York and Tokyo.

The interior has been crafted by the American architect to show art at its best. Neutral grey granite floors, translucent glass and white walls predominate. The gallery spaces flow one into the other, but they have been sculpted so that each is slightly different. The main entrance gallery is dominated by a full-width stair which glides down from light-filled spaces beyond. These are the rear galleries, lit from above by diffused daylight penetrating through glass blocks set in a precast-concrete frame. The spaces can be closed off for restricted shows, during receptions or when exhibitions are being prepared. A room off the main hall provides a more intimate space for smaller exhibits.

Offices are reached through stainless steel doors either side of the stair. The two wings are linked by a bridge which compresses the section over the stair and is enclosed with opaque and clear glass blocks.

Salamanca and Chamberí

ADDRESS Calle Orfila 5, 28010 Madrid
CLIENT Galería Marlborough SA
METRO Colón (line 4), Alonso Martínez (lines 4, 5, 10)
BUS 3, 7, 21
ACCESS Tuesday to Saturday 11.00–14.00, 17.00–21.00

Richard Gluckman 1992

Teatriz

It seems appropriate that Madrid, Europe's capital of the night, should be blessed with this restaurant/bar designed by the *enfant terrible* of nocturnal architecture, Philippe Starck. Teatriz is an orgy of contradiction and verve, and it never fails to impress.

The building was originally the Infanta Beatriz Theatre, designed by Eduardo Sanchez and Eduardo Lozaro in 1923. It was bought by Placido Arango, the owner of VIPS and BOBS, as a flagship for the restaurant/café/convenience store chain. Starck had already proved himself the maverick of interior design with Café Costes (Paris), Restaurant Manin (Tokyo) and the Royalton Hotel (New York). It was Ian Shrager, developer of the Royalton, who advised Arango to commission Starck.

The design works closely with the original architecture of the theatre, unfolding in flourishes from foyer to stage. The entrance is understated, with two fat, almost human, columns, white upholstered chairs and a pear-veneered bar only hinting at the adventure beyond. Grey leather padded doors entice clientele past this often empty foyer into a warmer, curving corridor surrounding the auditorium. The rest rooms, situated at either end of this space, give clues to the excitement to come: the basin in the men's toilet has a bent steel tube throwing water on to a solid marble block; in the women's toilet the basin is made of angled mirrors wildly flinging reflections in every direction.

There are two entrances into the dining room, neither of which prepares you for the drama. The round space preserves the full height of the theatre. A giant velvet curtain surrounds the upper levels and is pulled back at one point by a timber pole to reveal a balcony to the first-floor bar, like a box in the old theatre. The soffit of the surrounding balcony compresses the volume over perimeter tables, creating a sense of intimacy. The walls at this level are pear veneered, and the floor is painted with an

Philippe Starck 1989

Philippe Starck 1989

Salamanca and Chamberi

interpretation of De Chirico's *Two Sisters*, only comprehensible when seen from above.

On the stage, the back-lit onyx bar appears like a precious jewel. The aluminium stools, originally designed for the Royalton Hotel, face inwards, so that self-conscious customers do not feel too conspicuous sitting in such an exalted position. A mirror hanging from the wall gives depth to the space and is angled to show the reflection of onlookers in the first-floor bar. Above the stage, the original fly tower has been preserved, the crumbling brick illuminated by subtle spotlighting.

The downstairs bar, by contrast, is intimate and luxurious, with velvet upholstered furniture and pear veneers. Next to this space is a small, padded leather dance room with a thermally responsive floor which leaves a delayed shadow imprint of dancing feet.

The basement toilets alone justify a visit to Teatriz. Tiled toilet pods are arranged like pavilions behind etched-glass screens. Baroque marble tables form basins, with water outlets hidden in the legs. The entire space is bathed in blue UV light, and the ultra-cool 'Bladerunner' atmosphere is broken only by the excited giggles of a distinctly conservative clientele.

Starck believes Teatriz to be his most balanced work to date. Not surprisingly, it is also the slickest joint in town.

ADDRESS Calle Hermosilla 15, 28001 Madrid
CLIENT Sigma SL
GRAPHIC DESIGN Javier Mariscal
STAGE LIGHTING Arnold Chang
METRO Serrano (line 4) BUS 1, 74
ACCESS restaurant daily 13.30–16.00, 21.00–1.00; bars 21.00–3.00

Philippe Starck 1989

Salamanca and Chamberi

Philippe Starck 1989

Banco Santander Headquarters

When Banco Santander decided to move its headquarters from the AZCA development into three neighbouring nineteenth-century buildings on the Paseo de la Castellana, the bank's president Emilio Botín demanded 'the best architect in the world' to design the new offices. In a star-studded limited competition, entries were invited from Alvaro Siza, Rafael Moneo, Michael Graves and, the ultimate winner, Hans Hollein.

Hollein's work is in fact limited to the entrance hall and atria; the offices and subsidiary spaces were all designed by the bank's in-house architects.

Conservation and planning requirements meant that the exterior elevations of the three buildings and the form of the internal patios had to be retained. From the outside, the only indication of the dramatic interior spaces is the revolving glass entrance doors and the large vertical slab of granite embossed with the bank's name.

The marble-floored entrance hall is a cool, restrained space watched over by El Greco's *Adoration of the Shepherds*. The reception desk is formed by a sheet of glass supported on a steel beam and cantilevered from a solid granite block. A special fixing had to be developed to cope with the different coefficients of deflection of the canted glass and steel.

A bridge crosses the basement of the first patio and leads into the main atrium. It provides a real sense of a gateway, crossing into what must surely be one of the least known and most triumphant pieces of recent interior architecture in Spain. Cut-back marble panels on either side of the bridge separate the rectangular form of the patio from the widening conical atrium.

At basement level, a small fountain throws water into a pool, filling the atrium with the sound of splashing water. A sculptural stairway in stainless steel plate cantilevers off the wall and links the first and second floors. The circular rooflight allows sunlight to fill the atrium and seems

Hans Hollein 1993

Hans Hollein 1993

to hover within the overall square space. Hollein originally conceived the rooflight as a translucent shell, but it was eventually built with clear glass so that workers can see what the weather is like. The overlapping mesh baffles to the rooflight and the screens to the top three floors of the atrium are made of laton, an alloy of iron, copper and zinc.

At ground level, a stairway reaches out as if in greeting, its sinuous stainless steel handrail gliding up to the first floor. Balcony floors are finished in a green quartz from the Alpine Splugapass. The Clauzzetto cream marble used elsewhere is from Friuli in Italy.

The delight of these spaces is their variety. Apparent symmetries are offset by asymmetries and the rich palette of materials is so finely balanced that it never overawes.

On the top floor, a balcony cantilevers out from the presidential suite. When he looks down into the spaces below, Emilio Botin must think that perhaps he really did get 'the best architect in the world'.

ADDRESS Paseo de la Castellana 24, 28046 Madrid
CLIENT Banco Santander
EXECUTIVE ARCHITECT Alfonso Millanes of Banco Santander
AREA 20,000 square metres
METRO Ruben Dario (line 5) BUS 1, 5, 14, 27, 45, 74, 150
ACCESS none, but it is possible to see into the atrium from the
Banco Santander branch at Calle de Ortega y Gasset 1 (Monday to Friday
8.30–14.00; Saturday 8.30–13.00)

Hans Hollein 1993

Salamanca and Chamberi

Hans Hollein 1993

Fundación Carlos de Amberes

The Foundation was established in 1594 by Carlos Amberes, a Flemish aristocrat living in Spain. He set up a church and guest house for Flemish pilgrims in Calle de San Marcos. In 1877, the Foundation moved to its present premises, designed by Agustín and Manuel Ortiz de Villajos. The symmetrically planned facilities included a church, inn, hospital, meeting room, offices and rear patio. Solans, Briales and del Amo's design brings new life to the building, replacing the original facilities with a cultural centre. The façade and church are protected by building laws, so the architects have worked with them to create a series of new spaces to complement the old.

The work of the Villajos brothers was characterised by its human scale, contextual elevations, defined central space and aisles with flexibility for expansion. The redevelopment exploits these principles. The church has been restored with steel-framed transparent galleries added on either side. The three spaces are interconnected so that exhibitions can spread freely through the whole of the ground floor. Idiosyncratic red steel columns carry the polycarbonate glazed roofs, bursting through to provide lateral support to the church, like gothic flying buttresses.

The curved box which has been added to the back of the nave gives access to the café and lecture theatre, built beneath the rear patio. From this tree-shaded courtyard, the clear definition of elements is apparent.

ADDRESS Calle Claudio Coello 99, 28001 Madrid
CLIENT Fundación Carlos de Amberes
AREA 1500 square metres COST 300 million pesetas
METRO Núñez de Balboa (lines 5, 9) BUS 1, 74
ACCESS Tuesday to Friday 10.00–20.00

José Luis Solans, Pilar Briales and Ricardo del Amo 1992

Salamanca and Chamberí

Salamanca and Chamberi

José Luis Solans, Pilar Briales and Ricardo del Amo 1992

ABC Building

Three applications for planning permission were made for this shopping/restaurant project as the client enlisted first American and then British commercial property consultants to advise on layouts. In the end, Mariano Bayón persuaded his client to adopt a clear, rational approach, linking three existing buildings with one new structure.

The white stuccoed building facing Calle Serrano (1899, José López Sallaberry) has been painstakingly restored to provide a restaurant. It contains exquisite roof paintings and leaded rooflights in the Seville art nouveau style. Its timber structure has been invisibly reinforced with steel to cope with additional loadings. The ornate brick and tile façade of the building on Paseo de la Castellana (1926, Teodoro Anasagasti and Anibal Gonzalez) was once the front of the ABC newspaper works. Parallel to this, the third old building (1932, Teodoro Anasagasti), also part of the ABC print works, is set back but is much taller, a bold interpretation of 1920s Chicago School architecture.

Between these older buildings, Bayón has inserted a cool, restrained design organised around a three-storey atrium. An arched concrete roof held in tension by steel tie-rods spans the shopping mall. At roof level, a glass lift gives access to a café terrace with views over the treetops to Rafael Moneo's seminal Bankinter Headquarters (1973).

ADDRESS Calle Serrano 61/Paseo de la Castellana 34, 28006 Madrid
CLIENT Plataforma 61 SA
AREA 29,000 square metres COST 4000 million pesetas
METRO Rubén Dario (line 5), Núñez de Balboa (lines 5, 9)
BUS 1, 9, 19, 51, 74
ACCESS open

Mariano Bayón 1991–95

Mariano Bayón 1991–95

Crisol Bookshop, Aguilar Building

The rationalist Aguilar building, designed by Vicente Eced, was bought by Jesús del Polanco, the publishing mogul whose empire includes *El País*, the Santillana publishing house and the Librería Crisol chain. Allende's redevelopment creates five floors of offices for Santillana above the main Madrid branch of Crisol. It combines detail elements which recur at Allende's other Crisol bookshops at Calle Goya 18 and Paseo de la Castellana 154, and an organisation around an enclosed courtyard comparable to that of the Fundación Santillana at Calle Méndez Núñez 17.

The original façade forms an arcade at street level in front of the shop's glass front. The entrance to the offices is raised, reached by a folded-plate stair wedged between the shop window and brick piers. The bookshop is organised on a series of levels connected by galleries, stairs and ramps. Perforated steel panels undulate across the ceiling, hiding services. Spindly steel columns support galleries and uplighters. Steel display shelves are fixed on rollers so that they can be moved around the perimeter. The occasionally 'home-made' aesthetic blends well with tranquil classical music to create a relaxed environment in which to browse.

ADDRESS Calle Juan Bravo 37, 28006 Madrid
CLIENT Canal de Editoriales
TECHNICAL ARCHITECTS Fernando and Luis Pahissa
SERVICES ENGINEER Estudio de Consultores en Ingeniería de Instalaciones SA
COST 250 million pesetas
METRO Núñez de Balboa (lines 5, 9), Diego de Leon (lines 4, 6)
BUS 9, 19, 29, 51, 52
ACCESS Monday to Saturday 10.00–22.00; Sunday 11.00–15.00, 17.00–21.00

Gabriel Allende 1986–87

Salamanca and Chamberi

Gabriel Allende 1986–87

Velázquez Offices

On the corner of Calle Maria de Molina, this office building is clad in 30-millimetre-thick panels of grey granite from Extremadura, punctured by a grid of square double-glazed windows. The glazing units are made up of 10-millimetre green glass with a 6-millimetre clear plate inner leaf. On the west elevation, an additional green tempered glass screen is cantilevered off the main façade. Metal walkways on each floor provide transom support to the glass screen and give access for window cleaning. The horizontal edges of the glass are stuck to the steel walkways with structural bonding silicone; vertical joints are left open. Air can circulate between the glass and stone façade, giving offices extra insulation from extremes in temperature.

Contextually, Echevarría takes clues for his designs from buildings opposite – the elevations of this block relate to the grid of the Iberia offices across the road. Calle Maria de Molina marks one of the boundaries of the nineteenth-century Salamanca *barrio*, so it seems curious that he has related his design to a building from another generation across a wide avenue when the adjacent buildings offer a much stronger architectural context. The tightly curved corners are also a hallmark of his work – a reference to nineteenth-century Madrileño architecture in this area. But while the curved glass is of exceptional quality, the design of this corner is no match for the nineteenth-century corner *miradores* that can be seen on many neighbouring blocks.

ADDRESS Calle Velázquez 128, 28006 Madrid
CLIENT Hermanos Revilla SA
AREA 13,000 square metres COST 655 million pesetas
METRO Avenida de América (lines 4, 6, 7, 8, 9) BUS 9, 12, 19, 29, 51, 52
ACCESS none

Salamanca and Chamberí

Federico Echevarría 1987–88

Federico Echevarría 1987–88

Catalana Occidente Building

Along the Paseo de la Castellana there are a number of office buildings of quite outstanding quality. These include Rafael Moneo's Bankinter headquarters (1973), Corrales and Molezún's Bankunión building (1975), Sáenz de Oíza's Banco de Bilbao y Vizcaya (1980), Javier Carvajal's Adriática building (1981), Hans Hollein's Banco Santander headquarters (1993, see page 160), and this, one of the most under-rated buildings in the capital, a stunning essay in elegant cantilevers and structural glazing.

Set back from the Glorieta de Emilio Castelar on a grass embankment, it magnificently terminates the view down Calle General Martínez Campos. The elements of the brief were separated, with a low horizontal slab of meeting rooms, banking hall, staff areas and reception capped by an office tower. Both the horizontal block and the tower make maximum use of the structural potential of reinforced concrete to cantilever out, one plane floating above another. The resulting ghostliness is accentuated by an outer skin of tempered structural glazing, laminated to glass mullions with butyl silicone. The mullions are fixed back to the inner curtain wall of toughened reflective glass. The outer layer of glass lengthens the wavelength of the sun's infra-red rays, thus reducing solar penetration into the offices. It is separated from the inner layer so that heat escapes vertically.

The tower seems to defy gravity. The travertine-clad post-tensioned reinforced concrete core is asymmetrically positioned to avoid wasting circulation space. The floor area surrounding the core is formed in cantilevered reinforced concrete. The outer perimeter floor is made of steel plate hung on steel cables from the concrete roof slab. The core drops through a void in the horizontal building to a pool of water at basement level.

The building glides above a travertine platform reached by steps set

Rafael de la-Hoz 1977–86

Rafael de la-Hoz 1977–86

in the grass bank. The minimalist architecture has been stringently composed, making full use of technology while still applying the principles of contextualism and hierarchy – defining a bottom, middle and top to the building.

The constant changes in perception as sunlight is defracted at different angles through the outer glazed prism are mesmeric. This is a building that exhibits both urban and temporal contextuality, making it a rare example of 4D architecture.

Salamanca and Chamberi

ADDRESS Paseo de la Castellana 50, 28046 Madrid
CLIENT Banco Coca
STRUCTURAL AND SERVICES ENGINEERS OTEP Internacional
AREA 13,000 square metres COST 878 million pesetas
METRO Ruben Dario (line 5), Núñez de Balboa (lines 5, 9)
BUS 5, 7, 14, 16, 27, 40, 45, 61, 147, 150
ACCESS none

Rafael de la-Hoz 1977–86

Rafael de la-Hoz 1977–86

The British Council

When it became clear that this imposing nineteenth-century villa, containing the Council's school, needed to be refurbished, it was decided to relocate the administrative headquarters here (from the Plaza Santa Barbara), and move the school to the rear of the site.

Jestico+Whiles had previously worked for the British Council in Prague and were selected for the Madrid project to further the client's policy of synthesising their buildings worldwide. The Anglo-Spanish practice Reid Fenwick was invited to join them to assist with local building law and constructional technique. The finished product is, however, a truly Spanish collaboration in which the design represents a fusion of both practices' work.

Paths leading to offices and school are separated by a fence and a line of column-mounted lights. The grey finishes, deserted paved front space and security fences present an austere, almost forbidding face to the street, but once inside the villa opens out in unexpected ways.

Vertical distribution between floors has provided the key to the reorganisation. The ornate marble stair between the ground floor and the first floor has been retained, although the perforated steel ellipse set over the reception desk hints at something different above. This feeling is compounded by the glazed link to the arts department, housed in a low-quality extension which the architects have clearly separated from the villa with a plain render coat and an arched steel bridge set in a glass box.

The top floor is reached by an open-tread steel stair emerging into an elliptical opening. This elliptical cone constantly reduces in diameter down the building, with only one point on the south wall remaining constant. The off-centre rooflights are therefore visually linked to the central hall below. A mechanically controlled yellow fabric canopy

Jestico+Whiles with Reid Fenwick Asociados 1993

Salamanca and Chamberi

Jestico+Whiles with Reid Fenwick Asociados 1993

reduces solar gain through the rooflight. Hot air collected under the rooflight is expelled in summer and recycled in winter.

Steel and glass office partitions transfer light from rooflight to windows and vice versa. Original brick and concrete floors have been strengthened with a reinforced concrete screed and finished in public areas in beech, creating visual links between levels.

Increasingly, Spanish architecture fuses traditional and modernist idioms, but it is rarely that it marries Spanish and British design approaches – and certainly not as coherently as it does here.

ADDRESS Calle General Martínez Campos 31, 28010 Madrid
CLIENT The British Council
TECHNICAL ARCHITECT Luis Herrais
SERVICES ENGINEER CIASA
STRUCTURAL ENGINEER Alfonso Gómez Gaite
AREA 1800 square metres COST 207 million pesetas
METRO Iglesia (line 1), Ruben Dario (line 5) BUS 5, 16, 61
ACCESS none

Jestico+Whiles with Reid Fenwick Asociados 1993

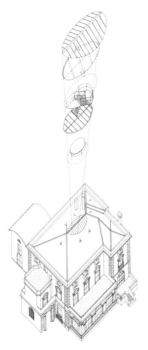

Jestico+Whiles with Reid Fenwick Asociados 1993

Advertising Columns

Madrid's street furniture mushroomed all over the city just before the 1995 municipal elections. It was supplied by El Imobilario Urbano SA, the Spanish arm of the French company J C Decaux, whose furniture had already taken over Valencia, Bilbao and Paris. The dominant elements are the plastic advertising columns, known in Madrid as *chirimbolos* (thingamajigs). They are dressed up to look like iron and decorated to appear a part of Madrid's heritage. There are more than 700 of them in the city and the *Ayuntamiento* justifies their presence on the basis of the advertising revenue they earn.

There are two types of *chirimbolo* in the capital. The least common, modern version, designed by Sir Norman Foster and Partners, is a clumsy composition of elegant shapes. It is little more than an overscaled bench covered by a canopy lifted up too high, which gives no shade and no shelter from the rain. The most common type is the 'Escorial' model, a name taken from the sixteenth-century palace in an attempt to suggest heritage and history. Festooned with mouldings and crawling with pastiche, the most ugly versions are those that assume some secondary function, such as a toilet or recycling bin. These components protrude like bloated bellies, the joint to the column shockingly unresolved.

The invasion of the *chirimbolos* has not been quietly accepted. In May 1995, 5000 people led by ETSAM professor Ricardo Aroca marched through the city to protest about this desecration of the streetscape. Unfortunately the columns remain.

ADDRESS throughout the city
CLIENT Ayuntamiento de Madrid
DESIGNERS J C Decaux, Sir Norman Foster and Partners and others

Salamanca and Chamberi

Salamanca and Chamberi

J C Decaux/El Imobilario Urbano SA 1995

Ciudad Universitaria

UNED Library

The Senda del Rey was the path that Spanish kings once took from the Royal Palace to their hunting grounds in the Montes del Prado. Tall American plane trees still grow along much of its length. The university library is next to the path, at the edge of the Ciudad Universitaria and overlooking the M30 motorway. The nearby Puente de los Franceses is the principal access point to central Madrid from Pozuelo, Aravaca and the Carretera de Castilla, making this a significant urban site.

The university rector Mariano Artes implemented the construction of three major new projects designed by Linazasoro, of which the library is the most emblematic (see pages 188 and 192). The building responds to the noise and pollution of the nearby motorway by turning in on itself. Only at the top does it open out to views of the Casa del Campo and the line of historic buildings strung along the western edge of the city.

Linazasoro describes his design as 'a book silo' – a powerful, strong container which provides an introverted place for study. In so doing, he has also created a building with a distinctly Spanish flavour. The library is clad in bricks from Toledo, laid with chalk mortar like the oldest university buildings, emphasising the classical, timeless context and symbolising stability.

The concrete structure is organised on a 4.5 x 4.5 metre grid independent of the external skin, and is expressed as a hypostyle hall at entry level. A glass screen offers a transparent division between the inside and the outside, with the travertine floor carrying through from one to the other. The horizontal slot windows at the far end of the hall give views of pine trees, but shut out the motorway. The sculptural screen at this level is by Christina Iglesias.

Stairs and lifts in opposite corners give oblique access to the six floors of book shelves and reading space – a device common to Hispano-Arabic

José Ignacio Linazasoro 1989–94

Ciudad Universitaria

José Ignacio Linazasoro 1989–94

palaces such as the Alhambra. The six-storey circular atrium on the first level comes as a dramatic surprise.

Although it has drawn comparisons with Louis Kahn's Exeter Library, the organisation of the space is entirely different. Here, books are placed on shelves around the perimeter, while readers sit at desks facing into the atrium, the heart of the building. The desks and balustrade are made of Oregon pine. Access stairs between levels are solidly detailed and air conditioning is provided by an isothermic system, all of which reduces distracting noises.

On the seventh floor, the atrium is cut back to a square beneath the coffered, laminated-timber ceiling of rooflights. These fill the atrium with a diffuse light, creating an atmosphere of concentration.

Above the reading levels, a floor of offices, meeting rooms and a café open out to panoramic views of Madrid and beyond. The café – which sadly is rarely open – has particularly good views from two sides.

ADDRESS Senda del Rey, Ciudad Universitaria, 28040 Madrid
CLIENT Ministerio de Educacion y Ciencia, Universidad Nacional de Educacion a Distancia
TECHNICAL ARCHITECTS Santiago Hernan and Juan Carlos Corona
AREA 8000 square metres COST 800 million pesetas
METRO Ciudad Universitaria (line 6) BUS 46
ACCESS Monday to Friday 9.00–20.00

José Ignacio Linazasoro 1989–94

Ciudad Universitaria

José Ignacio Linazasoro 1989–94

UNED Faculty of Economic Sciences and Business Studies

The site commands clear views over the busy M30 motorway into the Casa del Campo, the 4500-acre park to the west of Madrid. The design offers a clear organisation based, according to Linazasoro, on a comb. The spine contains access corridors, lifts and stairs, while the 'teeth' contain tutors' offices and classrooms separated by four patios. The patios have glazed façades to the back, blank precast concrete façades facing directly on to the motorway, and pale brick and glazed side elevations. The glazed façade is orientated towards the Casa del Campo, while the brick elevations face each other across the patios, turning away from the noise of the motorway. The patios are paved in travertine and covered by concrete canopies cut with an oculus. Throughout the day, circles of light cast into the patios constantly shift and change, much as they do in the Pantheon in Rome. The northernmost patio is raised to provide an outside seating area for a café and a roof to the lecture theatre below.

Internally, the building is economically finished in fairfaced concrete, painted brickwork and slate floors. As a result, Linazasoro has been able to concentrate on achieving a subtle repertoire of details in the elevational composition: expressed rebates between brick and concrete, a line of glass blocks between glass and concrete frame, and concrete canopies which appear to float above the patios.

ADDRESS Senda del Rey, Ciudad Universitaria, 28040 Madrid
CLIENT Universidad Nacional de Educacion a Distancia
TECHNICAL ARCHITECTS Santiago Hernan and Juan Carlos Corona
AREA 6000 square metres COST 660 million pesetas
METRO Ciudad Universitaria (line 6) BUS 46, 84, A
ACCESS during term time

José Ignacio Linazasoro 1994

Ciudad Universitaria

José Ignacio Linazasoro 1994

Ciudad Universitaria

Banco Central Hispano

The pavilion was originally constructed for the Fundacio Banco Central Hispano to display paintings at the 1992 Seville World Expo. It was subsequently sold to the Universidad Complutense and moved to Madrid. In a twist of fate, the original client is now the tenant.

In Seville, the pavilion stood on flat ground, but here the site falls steeply away into pine woods. A lower level has been added and glazing incorporated to take advantage of views of the trees. In Seville, Colomés created a windowless 'casket', politely deferring to larger neighbouring pavilions. Here in Madrid, the building is more transparent, mediating with its surroundings.

The concrete basement structure is arranged on a 6-metre grid and contains archives, exhibition space, toilets and plant room. Glass used in Seville to protect paintings has been reused to glaze the exhibition space. The upper level, which retains the original perimeter steel structure, is open plan, lit from above by circular rooflights. A linear window inserted in the east wall gives views of the surrounding landscape. This replaces the travertine panels of the original pavilion, which have been reused on the basement walls. In this way, no new cladding has been needed, even though the additional storey has been added.

The external composition draws inevitable comparisons with Mies van der Rohe's German pavilion for the Barcelona Expo (1929, reconstructed 1986).

ADDRESS Avenida Complutense, 28040 Madrid
CLIENT Universidad Complutense and Banco Central Hispano
AREA 800 square metres COST 102 million pesetas
METRO Ciudad Universitaria (line 6) BUS 1, 62, 82, 132, G
ACCESS open

Enrique Colomés 1993–95

Ciudad Universitaria

Enrique Colomés 1993–95

UNED Psychology Faculty

On the northern edge of the Zona Universitaria, this is a reinterpretation of Linazasoro's earlier work at the Faculty of Economic Sciences and Business Studies (see page 188). The scale, however, is much larger – even down to the brick dimensions – though the planning strategy is similar. Administration is organised in the linear brick block to the south, with teaching rooms, lecture theatre and library in four precast-concrete-clad wings divided by three patios. The base of the building is clad in rough-hewn Calatomo stone from Zaragoza, providing a muscular plinth. The patios are raised to take advantage of magnificent views over pine woods to the Sierra de Guadarrama. A rooflight set into each patio allows natural light into the car park below, increasing security.

The wings are divided from the administration block by a full-length slate-paved corridor, the walls to the offices finished in beech. Glazed curtain walls looking on to each patio allow light to flood into the corridor, while steel louvres prevent excessive heat gain. The lecture theatre and library are located in the west wing. With natural lighting pouring in from the side, the lecture theatre pays homage to Alvar Aalto's auditorium at Viipuri Library (1935). The two-level library is top-lit to prevent direct sunlight damaging the books. The shadows created on the interconnecting ramp constantly change and show off Linazasoro's skill at dramatically introducing natural light into rationalist plans.

ADDRESS Ciudad Universitaria, 28040 Madrid (near Facultad de Derecho)
CLIENT Universidad Nacional de Educacion a Distancia
AREA 12,000 square metres COST 1000 million pesetas
METRO Ciudad Universitaria (line 6) BUS 1, 62, 82, 83, 133, G, F
ACCESS during term time

Ciudad Universitaria

José Ignacio Linazasoro 1995

Ciudad Universitaria

José Ignacio Linazasoro 1995

Pozuelo to Las Matas

Pozuelo Police Station

The police station faces the well-maintained gardens of the Parque Fuente de la Salud. Its composition – employing functional expressionism and volumetric fragmentation to sculptural effect – is characteristic of Alvarez-Sala, Rubio Carvajal and Ruíz-Larrea.

The brief called for a building that would reflect an open, approachable image for the police. A concrete-framed rectangular block houses offices, its yellow rendered façade divided into horizontal panels by strips of aluminium. The core is expressed as a white box which emerges at the top of the building as a rooflight. Strips of horizontal windows are broken on one corner by a tile-clad secondary stair tower.

In front, a glazed pavilion emphasises the openness of the station by fanning out towards the street. The base of the pavilion is clad in lime-stone and the interior is timber panelled. Rubble-stone walls surround the complex, drawing into the composition the security guard's pill-box which is set beneath its own steel canopy.

The building is raised up on a grassy bank, concealing car parks and workshops behind. It also hides the secondary access for detainees. Despite the approachable image, be careful not to take photographs or look too intently at this building – you may be politely accompanied inside and asked to explain yourself.

ADDRESS Camino de las Huertas (opposite Parque Fuente de la Salud), Pozuelo, 28023 Madrid
CLIENT Dirección General de la Policia
TECHNICAL ARCHITECTS Vicente Arenas and Gonzalo García Loygorri
AREA 4200 square metres COST 515 million pesetas
METRO *cercanía* to Pozuelo (C7)
ACCESS none

Alvarez-Sala, Rubio Carvajal and Ruíz-Larrea 1991–92

Alvarez-Sala, Rubio Carvajal and Ruíz-Larrea 1991–92

Casa Turégano

This white cubic house stands in complete contrast to its brick and pitch-roofed neighbours. Unlike so many of Campo Baeza's poorly maintained public projects, Casa Turégano remains in good condition, showing off the architect's economic manipulation of Spanish tradition and international modernism to great effect.

The house is dug into the sloping site and divided by the east–west stair. The main rooms face south, while the kitchen, bathrooms and bedrooms look north. A study is above the double-height dining and living rooms. The three spaces are diagonally interconnected, so the study peers into the dining room which in turn looks over the sitting room. This organisation is reflected in the façades, closed to the north and opening out to the south to views over the Jardines de las Huertas below.

The flush glazing set in square openings relates to the square shape of the façades and the overall cubic form. Daylight plays a critical role and has been carefully exploited to connect spaces. The limestone floors absorb light while the white walls reflect it. The house exhibits all the discipline inherent in the modern movement while exuding the very essence of Spanish simplicity, as it merges into the landscape and is seen against the blue Madrileño sky.

ADDRESS Constantino Rodriguez 17, Colonia de las Minas, Pozuelo, 28023 Madrid
CLIENT Roberto Turégano
TECHNICAL ARCHITECT Gerado Berrocal
AREA 300 square metres COST 12 million pesetas
METRO *cercanía* to Pozuelo (C7) BUS 562, 563, 564, 656, 815
ACCESS none

Alberto Campo Baeza 1987–90

Alberto Campo Baeza 1987–90

Schoenstatt Institute

The Order of Our Lady of Schoenstatt was founded in 1914 outside Koblenz, Germany, expanding into Spain in 1960. There are now Schoenstatt convents in more than 150 countries and in each the original sanctuary has been faithfully reproduced. Wherever they are built, the chapels are sited in tranquil gardens. They attract large numbers of pilgrims.

The centre houses a 400-seat conference/prayer hall, three smaller meeting rooms, a social area, kitchen, dormitory and visitors' flat with separate access. A blockwork spine-wall of accommodation shuts the centre off from the noise of the road and the suburban wasteland beyond. It contains an office, kitchen, dormitory, flat and some underused terraces. The principal meeting spaces fan out from the spine in overlapping slices of pale brickwork. Clerestory glazing fills the rooms with sunlight. The glazed end wall of the main hall is orientated towards the sanctuary, sitting 200 metres away on a grassy hill. Congregations turn their backs on the sanctuary, facing instead the stage at the apex of the triangular room.

Traditional rough-hewn slate floors contrast with the otherwise industrial aesthetic. Allende and Ruíz Barbarín have limited their normally expressive steelwork detailing, imbuing spaces with greater architectural purity and ensuring that the diagrammatic logic of the plan remains clear.

ADDRESS Camino de Alcorcón 17, Pozuelo, 28023 Madrid
CLIENT Instituto Secular de Schoenstatt
TECHNICAL ARCHITECT Miguel Angel Muñoz
STRUCTURAL ENGINEER Eufemiano Sanchez
AREA 1300 square metres COST 90 million pesetas
METRO *cercanía* to Pozuelo (C7) BUS 657
ACCESS gardens open daily 7.00–22.00

Gabriel Allende and Antonio Ruíz Barbarín 1991–92

Gabriel Allende and Antonio Ruíz Barbarín 1991–92

Majadahonda Music School

The music school seems to spew out of the ground like a monstrous organism roused from slumber. Surrounding pools appear bottomless, so the emergent fractured elements of the building gain exaggerated potency, their brooding character in absolute contrast to their lifeless neighbours.

The insitu cast concrete and glass-block enclosure combine with dark-varnished oxidised steel to present an entirely deconstructivist composition. As in the Tesauro Offices (see page 224), Bellosillo's skill has been to rip the constituent parts ruthlessly apart while maintaining a thoroughly logical sequence of spaces. Circulation runs along a central spine. This carves through a cylinder at the southern end, dividing class and seminar rooms. The entrance, through a pivoting steel door, is perpendicular to the spine. The inclined auditorium crashes into the north-east side of this spine, and is entered next to a cascade of water.

Internal finishes continue the post-industrial imagery of the exterior. Grey granite floors, dark waxed-plaster walls and varnished steel make for an entirely apposite introversion. Bellosillo describes the building as being 'like hell', yet the wash of diffuse light, ever-changing perspectives and constantly reconnecting spatial experiences seem more celestial than infernal. Perhaps the architect is referring to the task of resolving so many complex constructional junctions.

ADDRESS Avenida de España, Calle las Norias, Majadahonda, 28230 Madrid
CLIENT Ayuntamiento de Majadahonda
AREA 3200 square metres COST 485 million pesetas
METRO *cercanía* to Majadahonda (C7) BUS 651, 652, 653, 654 (*interurbana* from Moncloa)
ACCESS none

Javier Bellosillo 1991–96

Javier Bellosillo 1991–96

Central Fire Station

The complex has two distinct functions: it serves as a fire station for the rural north of the Madrid district, and head offices for the capital's fire department. It is sandwiched between railway lines and the Carretera de la Coruña highway. Its clear geometric forms have been designed for instantaneous recognition as cars and trains pass by at high speed. The offices are contained in a cylinder and the fire station is overlooked by a training and communications tower. Larrucea's strategy has been successful and the complex has become a local landmark.

The buildings are on three levels, related to the sloping site. The brick cylindrical office block rests on a Rosa de Porriño granite arcade. Offices have views either of the landscape or into the triple-height atrium which cuts the building in two. The top-lit atrium is flanked by linear stairs, layering the internal façades. A precast-concrete aedicule at the entrance holds a processional stair leading up to the first floor. At the opposite end, the lift and escape stairs are enclosed in a brick cylinder expressed on the elevation. The relationship of circulation cylinder to cylindrical building is a powerful device inherited from Mario Botta.

The design of the fire station is based on pragmatism, with garages and workshops facing each other across a central space. This separation enables vehicles to leave from the west within 20 seconds of the fire alarm sounding, and to return to the east to be refilled and prepared.

ADDRESS Carretera Nacional VI, Las Rosas, 28230 Madrid
CLIENT Comunidad de Madrid
AREA 9693 square metres COST 780 million pesetas
METRO *cercanía* to Pinar (C8) BUS 622 (interurbana from Moncloa)
ACCESS none

Pozuelo to Las Matas

Francisco Larrucea 1987–89

Francisco Larrucea 1987–89

Caja de Madrid Offices

Driving out of Madrid on the N-VI, the views into the Casa del Campo are quickly restricted by the relentless roadside development of anti-urban commercial blocks. The Parque Empresarial Las Rozas, begun in the early 1990s, would have extended this theme further into the countryside, but the development failed to take root and the land, criss-crossed by roads and street lamps, is all but empty of offices. But one project has been constructed, facing directly on to the motorway, and it is one of the most innovative and elegant of Madrid's recent commercial buildings.

The Caja de Madrid, the city's largest bank, wanted to rationalise its numerous offices into one centre. Junquera, Pérez-Pita and Obal's design provides 20,000 square metres of office space, a vast information technology centre and 20,000 square metres of parking. Virtually all visitors and employees arrive by car, and this determined the organisation. Rather than separating cars and pedestrians, the entrance combines them. A wide avenue cuts across the west of the site, from which a ramp descends beside a pool to the hypostyle entrance hall and drop-off zone. Vehicles turn back from here to a series of parking levels beneath lavender-planted terraces, daylight flooding into the garages through the gaps between each terrace. The manipulation of the sloping site disguises the array of equipment housed underground. From the motorway the Caja de Madrid appears as a sleek three-storey container, yet stretching below ground to the west is another building filled with plant. At the western extreme the installations building opens on to a service yard, the elevational composition reflecting the abstracted Mondrianesque pattern of the office façades.

The office block focuses on two protected 27-metre-square patios and a circular atrium, all rising above the basement-level entrance hall. Sunlight, filtered through horizontal clear Climalit glass, penetrates to the bottom of each of these volumes. Structural silicone-glazed curtain walls

Jerónimo Junquera, Estanislao Pérez-Pita and Liliana Obal 1992–96

Jerónimo Junquera, Estanislao Pérez-Pita and Liliana Obal 1992–96

give uninterrupted views into the patios, the elevations stepping in at the upper level to form a perimeter walkway. Giant lateral and longitudinal steel gutter beams span the patios. Glass is raised above the beams to allow natural ventilation of the voids. At the southern end of the block the floor level of the patio is raised to cover the computer centre, glass-block walls bathing the machinery in a subdued, diffuse light.

The 16-metre clear structural span of the offices permits a limitless flexibility with varied views out and into the building through the carefully composed façades. These reflect the architects' interest in layering the components of construction.

The rigorous structural grid is clad in flamed black Zimbabwe granite. The infill panels of velvety Bernardos slate and Luxguard glass are conceived as independent curtain walls. The panels are arranged in three modules which repeat in diagonals across the façades, creating an intriguingly uniform but patchwork effect. On the south, east and west façades the panels are set back from the grid, further protected by glass canopies, but to the north they are pulled forward to match the plane of the granite.

Modern architecture often attracts poor press for its blandness and denigration of craftsmanship. Here, sophistication and subtlety are married to a delightful feel for materials, detail and technology to forge a building at once human in scale and giant in stature.

ADDRESS Calle Gabriel Garcia Marquez 1, Parque Empresarial Las Rozas, Las Rozas, 28230 Madrid
AREA 60,000 square metres
STRUCTURAL ENGINEER Alfonso Gómez Gaite
METRO *cercanía* to Pinar (C8) BUS 622 (*interurbana* from Moncloa)
ACCESS none

Jerónimo Junquera, Estanislao Pérez-Pita and Liliana Obal 1992–96

Pozuelo to Las Matas

Jerónimo Junquera, Estanislao Pérez-Pita and Liliana Obal 1992–96

Casa Rodríguez

This is the second house designed by Vicens and Ramos for the Rodríguez family. The first involved the reordering of a 1940s colonial-style house at Key Biscayne, Miami (1988–89).

When Gonzalo Rodríguez, a financier, and his wife, the daughter of a city politician, bought this plot in the exclusive Urbanizacion del Golf, they gave the architects a virtual free hand.

Seen from the twisting roads which lead from the Carretera de la Coruña, the house stands out and yet seems to sink down into its setting: long, low and the colour of earth, its form has been moulded to become part of the landscape. The roots of this contextuality lie in a marriage between modernist principles and traditional idioms. At one moment the house evokes Le Corbusier or Luis Barragán, the next it calls to mind the robust and earthy homesteads of Castille y Leon.

Planting around the house is compatible with the surrounding landscape of pines and scorched earth. Against this background, the manicured lawn and floodlit football pitch seem strangely out of place. The rendered concrete façades have been stained with iron sulphate, giving them a textured, rusty appearance. The elements that protrude from the two-storey central section – the rooflight, front door, main bedroom, office and a hall window – are clad in varnished, oxidised sheet steel.

The clients' main requirement – to separate parents' accommodation from that of the six children – became the starting point for the project. The parents' bedroom, father's study, mother's office, living accommodation and kitchen occupy a two-storey central core. Children's rooms, a television room, indoor pool, covered terrace and covered parking are arranged on either side in linear wings which burrow into the hillside.

The double-height entrance hall draws light from above like an internal courtyard. The floating of volumes within a large container has become

Ignacio Vicens and José Antonio Ramos 1991–92

Ignacio Vicens and José Antonio Ramos 1991–92

a hallmark of Vicens and Ramos' work, and has been magnificently manipulated here. The mother's office is like a look-out, reached by a bridge. It protrudes from the central core to give views both into the garden and of the entrance. The parents' bedroom is perpendicular to this axis. It hovers over the living area and cantilevers out over the lawn. A window frames views from the bed of landscape and sky. The bedroom lowers the scale over part of the living room to create an intimate television watching area, surrounded by an oxidised steel screen with incised back-lit recesses for ceramics – a homage to Le Corbusier's chapel at Ronchamp. The more formal sitting area is double height.

Children's accommodation is organised along the north wing. Small patios separate the playroom, bathroom and nanny's room, and bring daylight into the corridor. The children share the bathroom, which is as fastidiously minimalist as all the other rooms in the house.

Details and materials are consistent with the overall architectural tone: parchment-coloured walls, polished concrete floors, oxidised steel door frames and MDF kitchen units. With their simple geometries and small indigo-tiled finishes, even the two swimming pools achieve a counterpoise between modern minimalism and Castilian tradition.

ADDRESS Calle Cabo Finisterre 4, Urbanizacion del Golf, Las Matas, 28290 Madrid
CLIENT Gonzalo Rodríguez Fraile
AREA 817 square metres COST 89 million pesetas
METRO *cercanía* to Las Matas (C8) then 25-minute walk
BUS 611, 622, 664, 671, 672, 682, 683, 684 (interurbana from Moncloa to Las Matas on the N-VI Carretera de La Coruña), then 25-minute walk
ACCESS none

Ignacio Vicens and José Antonio Ramos 1991–92

Ignacio Vicens and José Antonio Ramos 1991–92

Ciudad Lineal to Chamartín

Santa Maria y Santa Isabel Retirement Home

After they had trained in Alberto Campo Baeza's unit at ETSAM, this was the first project built by husband and wife team Juan Carlos Sancho and Sol Madridejos, working with the more experienced Ignacio Vicens. Their design for the retirement home exhibits characteristics that recur in the work of both practices: double-skin façades, entrance patios, indirect sources of daylight and the positioning of geometric forms in space (in this case, a cylindrical lift shaft).

On a sloping site, the building contains accommodation for 40 elderly residents in full-time nursing care, a dining room, communal areas and ancillary services. The entrance is signalled by a concrete canopy supported at one corner by a column. A bridge cuts through an acute façade and a full-height glazed screen to give access to a double-height entrance space which is animated by the lift cylinder and concrete ramps with black steel panel balustrades. The ramps puncture curved communal landing areas at each level. The entrance hall achieves a sense of great spaciousness in a limited area, providing a heart to the building. Views from the fully glazed bedrooms are framed by square openings punched into the outer limestone skin. This secondary façade wraps the building, protecting it from an otherwise disintegrated urban environment.

ADDRESS Calle Ulises 60, 28043 Madrid
CLIENT Fundación Santa Maria y Santa Isabel
TECHNICAL ARCHITECT José Ramon Parrondo
AREA 1000 square metres COST 120 million pesetas
METRO Arturo Soria (line 4) BUS 120, 122
ACCESS none

Juan Carlos Sancho, Sol Madridejos and Ignacio Vicens 1990, 1994

Ciudad Lineal to Chamartín

Juan Carlos Sancho, Sol Madridejos and Ignacio Vicens 1990, 1994

Toronga Housing

Domínguez has emphasised the linearity of this long, narrow site, placing a car park at one end and a playground at the other. Six floors contain 32 housing units above two levels of office and commercial space and one level of underground parking. None of the office space is let and only one retail unit is occupied. This leaves the base of the building lifeless, creating a sense of isolation at the end of the street – a shame, because the architect has manipulated simple materials and disciplined geometries to form an extremely well thought out organisation and elevational treatment.

Access is arranged along the north side, with balconies to apartments along the south, taking advantage of sunlight and panoramic views of the east side of Madrid. When construction had reached the third-floor level, the client requested a reorganisation of the plan to include one- and four-bed apartments alongside the two- and three-bed flats already designed. Domínguez has achieved this by reorientating bathrooms and duplex stairs.

Plants, patio furniture and drying washing bring life to the south-facing balconies and counterpoint the scale of the brick framework. At ground level, semicircular windows cut into the solid brick base convey a sense of strength, so that the building appears like a fortified tower overlooking the city. The north façade is a reverse of the south, with closed linear galleries and an open portico.

ADDRESS Calle Toronga 31, 28043 Madrid
CLIENT Empresa Municipal de la Vivienda
AREA 5000 square metres COST 160 million pesetas
METRO Esperanza (line 4) BUS 120, 122
ACCESS none

Martín Domínguez 1988–90

Martín Domínguez 1988–90

Badajoz Housing

This housing project was the first to be built in the *barrio* of La Alegría. Its 130 units are organised in a linear block flanked by two towers, the gaps between them relating to openings in the developments behind. The towers give formality to the elevation on to Avenida de Badajoz, announcing entry into the new *barrio*. Retail units at ground level have been fully let and add life to this leafy street.

Central courtyards bring light into the heart of each building – there are three in the linear block and one in each tower. Where possible, living rooms are planned on the diagonal of the courtyards, giving a double aspect to the apartments in the towers and those on the corners of the linear block. Kitchens and bathrooms face into the courtyards, filling them with the noise of cooking, clanking plates and running water.

The concrete-framed structure is clad in brick, with bands of precast concrete inserted at floor and mid-floor levels, emphasising the scheme's horizontality and directing rainwater away from the brickwork. Meanwhile verticality is emphasised by the window openings and cut-back asphalted corners. It is exaggerated still further on the towers by a two-storey set-back maisonette level crowned by a steel grille canopy supported on a concrete ring beam and columns.

Pedestrian access to the underground car park is via neat steel-framed pavilions set between the buildings. They incorporate a bench and are a small piece of sculptural design which transcends the purely functional.

ADDRESS Avenida de Badajoz 50–60, 28027 Madrid
CLIENT Empresa Municipal de la Vivienda
TECHNICAL ARCHITECT Martín Ramirez
METRO B Concepción (line 7) BUS 11, 53
ACCESS none

Javier Frechilla and José Manuel López-Pelaez 1986–88

Javier Frechilla and José Manuel López-Pelaez 1986–88

Funerary Centre

Bodies are brought here for embalming and for family and friends to pay their last respects. Red-profiled steel barrel-vaulted roofs and precast concrete panelled façades give an austere, even brutal, appearance to this building on the banks of the M30 motorway. The symmetrical plan is organised around a central courtyard with offices for the 700 staff placed in three- and four-storey buildings at either end. The 26 sets of funeral rooms are entered either from the courtyard or from two internal side 'streets'. Each set of rooms contains two sitting areas, one of which looks through a glass screen into the open coffin chamber. There are various sizes of sitting room to accommodate different family numbers.

Despite the austerity of the materials and the rigorous plan form, the scale of the external spaces is both dignified and peaceful, offering tranquillity and giving mourners the opportunity to sit inside or retire out into the sun. A café and staff restaurant are at basement level next to a car park for the silver Peugeot 505 hearses. The client – the *Ayuntamiento* – made a positive decision not to use black hearses, considering them unnecessarily macabre.

More recently, a much larger 60-room funeral building has been built beside the Carretera de Toledo to the south of Madrid, its mellow brick façades rather less brutal and imposing than the cold grey concrete employed here.

ADDRESS Calle Salvador de Madariaga 11, 28027 Madrid
CLIENT Ayuntamiento de Madrid
AREA 59,500 square metres COST 580 million pesetas
METRO Parque Avenidas (line 7) BUS 53
ACCESS none

Antonio Fernandez Alba 1984

Antonio Fernandez Alba 1984

Tesauro Offices

Tesauro's offices and video production studios present one of the more extraordinary examples of recent building in Madrid. Bellosillo's brand of deconstructivism makes a total break from the formalist tradition which dominates the city's architecture.

The studios are at the rear, inserted in an old two-storey industrial building and separated from the offices facing on to Calle Bocángel by stairs and a system of folded, varnished steel-plate galleries. The separation is emphasised by a glass enclosure, angled at 45 degrees over the stairs. The office building has also been remodelled. A screen protrudes from the façade, protecting slithers of balconies, creating an arcaded entrance and forming shadows. Behind the screen, glazed openings, oxidised steel and render have been meshed together into a patchwork over which a steel circle is superimposed. This circle binds the façade together and threads through the offices to reappear embedded in the internal elevations either side of the stair.

Internally, spaces are logically organised, creating order out of mayhem. Complicated joints, oversailing elements and angled steelwork suggest chaos, but as one part of the building seems to be pulled apart so another draws the composition together. The architecture is at once animated and rationally organised. The rusty steel, render sparkling with silicone additives, limestone floors and glass make a thrilling combination of materials.

ADDRESS Calle Bocángel 26, 28028 Madrid
CLIENT Tesauro SA
AREA 2025 square metres COST 180 million pesetas
METRO Ventas (lines 2, 5) BUS 12
ACCESS none

Javier Bellosillo 1989–93

Museo Nacional de Ciencias Naturales

The beaux-arts brick building (1881, Fernando de la Torriente) originally housed the Exposición de la Industria y las Artes. The steel frame was imported from Belgium. Subsequently it was split in two, with the museum taking the north wing and part of the south. Alau and Lopera's transformation of the north wing followed an earlier project to create a visitor centre at the Sala del Canal Isabel II (Calle Santa Engracia 125).

The entrance leads directly into the main hall, which is used for temporary exhibitions. The original structure has been maintained. Walkways have been added at first-floor level, compressing the height over circulation areas. The ecology rooms, installed in 1994, were designed by Victor Alarcon. Interactive displays fill the rooms with noise and energy.

The principal intervention is the round two-storey pavilion 'El Museo del Museo', sited in a courtyard and connected to the main building by a two-storey skeletal steel and glass enclosure. The glass roof extends to form a linear rooflight to the first floor of the pavilion. The ground floor is lowered and the first floor cut back, creating a light and spacious feel within a compact volume. The roughness of the exposed cast concrete structure contrasts with the smoothness of the white plastered suspended ceilings and the intricacy of the metallic steel and glass balustrades.

The juxtaposition of the boldly detailed architecture and the moth-eaten exhibits makes for an enticing display. Spatial control, dynamic form and light matter more than fussily detailed fixings or finishes.

ADDRESS José Gutierrez Abascal 2, 28006 Madrid
CLIENT Ministerio de Educacion y Ciencia
METRO República Argentina (line 6) BUS 7, 12, 14, 27, 40, 45, 147, 150
ACCESS Tuesday to Friday 10.00–18.00; Saturday 10.00–20.00;
Sunday 10.00–14.30

Javier Alau and Antonio Lopera 1990

Javier Alau and Antonio Lopera 1990

Castellana Offices 1

This office block (1972, Ricardo Magdalena) was a precast-concrete-clad stump until the Abu Dhabi Investment Agency decided to glitz it up. The building has come a long way from those ignominious beginnings, but that does not make it any easier to condone its current architecture.

Verticality has been emphasised in the tower, creating a landmark at the crossing of the Calle de Joaquin Costa fly-over and Paseo de la Castellana. There is a tenuous link with the towers in the AZCA development opposite, though the closest of these, the Banco de Bilbao y Vizcaya tower (1980, Sáenz de Oíza), commands more attention.

The horizontality of the neighbouring building is terminated with the layering of a protruding bay on the tower. The connection of this bay to the adjacent structures lacks conviction and is dominated by the glazing mullions and vertical travertine of the tower. Oversized stainless steel fins placed at the top of the elevation are intended to cap the building, but merely embellish the commercial imagery.

The most positive attribute is the minimalist crown; here, plant is kept out of view by travertine parapets. The pyramid glass cap unexpectedly encloses a meeting room which has a stunning 360-degree view – surely one of the best meeting spaces in Madrid.

ADDRESS Paseo de la Castellana 110, 28046 Madrid
CLIENT Abu Dhabi Investment Agency
PROJECT MANAGERS Deacon and Jones
AREA 10,000 square metres COST 1500 million pesetas
METRO Nuevos Ministerios (lines 6, 8, C1, C7, C8)
BUS 7, 14, 27, 40, 42, 147, 150, C
ACCESS none

Rafael de la-Hoz 1992–94

Rafael de la-Hoz 1992–94

Torre Picasso

The original designs for Madrid's tallest office building were prepared by Minoru Yamasaki, architect of the twin towers of the World Trade Center, New York (1973). Work was suspended in 1984 when the client, Explosivos Riotinto, suffered serious financial problems and the architect died. The project was eventually brought back to life and became the dominant silhouette on Madrid's skyline.

The 43 storeys of offices sit above five basement levels and are capped by two storeys of plant space and a heliport. The building is planned on a 1.5 x 1.5 metre grid with every component size a factor of this dimension – 3 metres between perimeter steel columns, 1.5-metre-square suspended ceiling panels, and so on. Externally, aluminium cladding alternates with vertical bronze glazed strips. A curved cornice caps the tower, while the three-storey solid-clad base conveys a sense of strength; the arched glazed entrance reinforces this impression. The 18 lifts are designed for use by 6000 people per day. The paving to the plaza in front is patterned to reflect the arched entry. The gardens to the south are full of shade, made cooler by splashing fountains. However, the underground approaches to the tower are dark, smelly and unwelcoming.

ADDRESS Plaza Pablo Ruíz Picasso, 28020 Madrid
CLIENT Comunidad de Proprietarios
TECHNICAL ARCHITECTS Carlos Carulla, J Antonio López Traveso and Francisco Rodríguez Regueira
STRUCTURAL ENGINEER Fernando Cid García
AREA 116,000 square metres COST 14,000 million pesetas
METRO Lima (line 8) BUS 5, 27, 40, 147, 149, 150
ACCESS atrium only

Minoru Yamasaki 1974, Alas Casariego Arquitectos 1985–88

Minoru Yamasaki 1974, Alas Casariego Arquitectos 1985–88

Santiago Bernabeu Stadium

Real Madrid is one of the world's great football clubs. In many of the city's bars, the team's results are the sole topic of conversation. Estudio Lamela's extension to the club's stadium reinforces this sporting gravitas with a thoroughly muscular concrete structure.

The original stadium was designed by Manuel Muñoz and José Alemany (1944–47) with a capacity for 75,000 spectators. Various changes in appearance and capacity followed, culminating in 1980, prior to the 1982 World Cup, when the stadium was re-clad, re-roofed and reorganised, giving it a capacity of 86,000.

Estudio Lamela was commissioned in 1988 to extend the capacity to 106,000 to meet increasing demand for tickets. To comply with regulations for international football competitions, the stadium had to be an all-seater with high standards of security, circulation and servicing.

To reduce costs, the original roof was retained and raised, using a computer-controlled lifting system. The upper levels are reached by four corner towers which feed into a high-level perimeter gallery. From here, secondary stairs, enclosed by concrete semi-cylinders suspended between alternate structural bays, lead to seating. The counterbalance of sturdy concrete and gymnastic cantilevers gives a kinetic form to the stadium.

ADDRESS Paseo de la Castellana/Calle Concha Espina, 28046 Madrid
CLIENT Real Madrid Club de Fútbol
STRUCTURE OTEP Internacional
SPORTS CONSULTANTS Oficina Tecnica Gines Navarro and Hotelpro
AREA 39,000 square metres COST 4800 million pesetas
METRO Lima (line 8) BUS 14, 27, 40, 43, 120, 147, 150
ACCESS match days only – check local press

Estudio Lamela 1991–93

Estudio Lamela 1991–93

Auditorio Nacional de Música

The concert hall's austere, formal brick and Colmenar limestone façades rest on a granite base and disguise the dramatic interiors. The building subtly reveals itself in layers – from the outside, only the protruding stone-clad volumes of the Sala Sinfónica and the Sala Cámara at roof level hint at the spatial drama to be found inside.

Entrances are positioned at either end of the building. The broken pediment over the entrance to the Sala Sinfónica assumes classical proportions, facing on to an amphitheatrical plaza. The triple-height foyer is flanked by processional stairs and flooded with natural light. The entrance to the Sala Cámara is lower key, set behind brick piers beneath the first-floor foyer. This entrance too faces on to an open space, the architect conscious of the urban role of this important building.

Circulation takes up the perimeter, providing an acoustic buffer which absorbs noise from the street. Cafés, kitchens, toilets, changing rooms, rehearsal rooms and offices surround the auditoriums. White plastered walls, pink granite and walnut panelling combine to create a tranquil atmosphere which is distinctly Scandinavian in its simplicity. The spaces are full of natural light, diffused through muslin blinds to recessed windows. Corbusian armchairs are formally arranged along the flanks to provide a tranquil area to relax in before performances or during the interval. A sculpture and tapestries by Eusebio Sempere and another sculpture by Julio López Hernandez can be seen in these areas.

The design of the 200-seat Sala Sinfónica has been driven by acoustics. The walnut ceilings curve and cascade down towards the stage. Angled and curved balconies diffuse and deflect sound as they dip downwards. The section is constantly varied and bursts into life during a concert. Acoustic definition is so clear that even during the loudest of movements it is possible to distinguish each instrument.

José Maria García de Paredes 1984–88

José María García de Paredes 1984–88

The concert hall is the home of the Orquesta y Coro Nacionales de España, whose performances are always extremely popular events. It is difficult to imagine a better start to a Sunday in Madrid than drinking a cup of coffee in the bright, cool café, being escorted to your seat by uniformed ushers and then surrendering to the swelling strains of the music.

Ciudad Lineal to Chamartín

ADDRESS Calle Príncipe de Vergara 146, 28002 Madrid
CLIENT Ministerio de Cultura, INAEM
ACOUSTIC CONSULTANT Lothar Cremer
AREA 25,000 square metres COST 2300 million pesetas
METRO Cruz del Rayo (line 9), Prosperidad (line 4) BUS 1, 52, 29
ACCESS for concerts (check local press)

José Maria García de Paredes 1984–88

José Maria García de Paredes 1984–88

Tetuan and Fuencarral

Alejandro Rodríguez Housing

Fresh out of ETSAM and aged only 27, Enrique Colomés won the competition to design this housing block. The building is set in an area of mixed public and private developments surrounded by well-maintained gardens and quiet streets. The basic floor plan of the concrete-framed, brick-clad building measures 20 x 12 metres, and each floor contains three apartments. Bathrooms, kitchens and vertical circulation are grouped along a central spine, with bedrooms and living areas facing outwards. One apartment on each floor has a double aspect. On the upper levels there are clear views of the Sierra de Guadarrama to the north-west of Madrid.

The south façade is animated by a curved plane protruding from the block and creating balconies behind – one geometrical form imposed upon another. The scale of the windows in the curve relates both to the proportions of the glazed openings in the rectangular block and the grid of the building's structural frame. Colomés enjoys the detailing of buildings and often expresses construction technique as a part of his architectural repertoire – in this case using the curved brickwork cladding to create sculptural impact.

The curve rests on a solid base, emphasising the dynamic form and giving a feeling of strength to the building. The north façade betrays nothing of the curve on the south side. The entirely regular grid of window openings lacks any elevational hierarchy and could easily be missed.

ADDRESS Calle Alejandro Rodríguez 37, 28039 Madrid
CLIENT Empresa Municipal de la Vivienda
AREA 2280 square metres COST 88 million pesetas
METRO Estrecho (line 1) or Cuatro Caminos (line 1) then bus 127, 128
BUS 127, 128
ACCESS none

Enrique Colomés 1987–89

Enrique Colomés 1987–89

Cactus Apartments

The *barrio* of Berrugete is made up of narrow streets with a mix of small-scale residential and commercial buildings. This neat design for two apartments and a maisonette offers a thoroughly modern example of the genre. The site is long and thin, and the architects have had carefully to manipulate the building's cross section to enable development of the greatest volume possible, and to permit daylight penetration. Steel columns have been placed on the site perimeter, with reinforced beams spanning the width of the site between. This has allowed maximum flexibility in the layout, allowing for the creation of vertical voids and patios.

The pastel green rendered façade on to Calle Cactus is subtly composed, relating both to the scale of the neighbouring buildings and the functions of spaces behind. The two lower levels of accommodation and the garage are placed to one side, separated from the vertical wall of the stair tower by a void at each alternate stair flight. The steel and glass stair is capped by a curved steel roof. A gridded and galvanised steel-framed screen to the garage and the first two apartments appears like an abstract painting, another device used to sew the building into the patchwork of designs and details along the street. At third-floor level, the façade to the maisonette is set back so that it does not interfere with the street composition.

A little gem, the building is exquisitely detailed – not surprisingly perhaps, since it is the home of one of the architects, César Ruíz-Larrea.

ADDRESS Calle Cactus 29, 28039 Madrid
CLIENT José Manuel Pombo Semprún (Inmocrimuz SL)
AREA 500 square metres COST 40 million pesetas
METRO Tetuán (line 1) BUS 42, 124, 125
ACCESS none

Alvarez-Sala, Rubio Carvajal, Ruíz-Larrea 1991–92

Alvarez-Sala, Rubio Carvajal, Ruíz-Larrea 1991–92

KIO Towers

Madrid boasts some of the best of Spain's recent architecture, but with the Torres KIO it stoops to the very worst. Alarmingly, the two towers, tilted at 15 degrees from the vertical, have become a symbol of the new Spain, often used as a backdrop for television news reports. For many years, Madrid has shown a greater fondness for America than other Spanish cities; the ignorant commercial response of New York architects Burgee and Associates to one of the prime sites in the capital shows how misguided this fascination can be.

The project, originally commissioned by the Kuwaiti Investment Office (KIO), has been fraught with problems and financial scandals. At one point the project was abandoned, and the shell of the towers remained in limbo until bought by the current owners.

The tilt is achieved by an inelegant steel structure, unimaginatively expressed in aluminium. The Robertson curtain wall cladding in black mirror glass is static, the small opening windows totally out of character with the commercial air-conditioned image. At ground level, a 32-metre geyser spouts water from a 50-metre-diameter pond, offset from the two entrance halls and dominated to the point of insignificance by the towers.

Americans need not bother travelling to Madrid to see these towers. They are an exact replica of an earlier development in Toledo, Ohio.

ADDRESS Plaza de Castilla, 28046 Madrid
CLIENT Kuwaiti Investment Office and (subsequently) Produsa
EXECUTIVE ARCHITECTS T Domínguez del Castillo and J C Martin Baranda
METRO Plaza de Castilla (lines 1, 8, 9)
BUS 5, 27, 42, 49, 66, 67, 70, 80, 124, 125, 129, 134, 135, 147, 149
ACCESS none

Burgee and Associates 1990–96

Tetuan and Fuencarral

Burgee and Associates 1990–96

Castellana Offices 2

At the point where the Paseo de la Castellana changes from tree-lined avenue to urban freeway, a series of new offices have been built. This block shines out both for its immaculate black aluminium and glass curtain wall and its dramatic entrance.

The wings of the building are joined by a bridge of offices carried above the entrance on steel trusses spanning between central columns and the cores. The latter, clad in precast concrete panels and aluminium louvres, frame the elevations and articulate the corners of the development. The offices are entered through a glass and steel box which pokes up like a periscope. Sunken semi-glazed corridors connect the entrance to the cores. From the Paseo de la Castellana, these subterranean passages are crossed by exquisitely detailed steel bridges which lead into an open space behind, creating a physical and visual link between road and plaza.

While the plaza is currently exposed to sun and roads, in time it will be shaded by trees and enlivened by water.

The simple concept, bold detailing and immaculate construction mark this out as one of Gabriel Allende's most convincing projects, creating urban space out of a hostile environment. The REPSOL building opposite (1992, Federico Echevarría, Paseo de la Castellana 146) retains the steel bones of the previous occupant, wrapped in a two-ply energy-efficient glazed skin.

ADDRESS Paseo de la Castellana 257, 28046 Madrid
CLIENT Aresbank
AREA 23,500 square metres COST 2100 million pesetas
METRO Chamartin (line 8, C1, C7, C8)
BUS 42, 66, 67, 80, 124, 125, 134, 135, 147
ACCESS none

Gabriel Allende 1991–94

Alejandro de la Sota Building

The Fuencarral B social housing project was masterplanned by Alejandro de la Sota in the 1950s and is now being redeveloped. This competition-winning project was selected from seven schemes (others were submitted by López Cotelo, Cano Lasso and Juan Montes) to provide both an emblematic building at the apex of Fuencarral and a homage to de la Sota.

The glazed, angled prow is extremely dynamic. There is clear vertical differentiation between housing and commercial space. While office and retail units placed beneath housing so often remain unlet, leaving ground floors dead, here the architects have devised an attractive solution likely to appeal to commercial tenants: their design not only provides the commercial component with its own distinct identity but also gives it uninterrupted views towards central Madrid.

Cores are expressed in glass block and protrude above the cantilevered steel cornice. The 84 apartments are rendered with strip glazing which emphasises horizontality. As with Araujo and Nadal's block on Calle Arroyo de la Media Legua (see page 50), bedrooms face on to the road, while living rooms have a more open aspect over waste ground, their balconies providing three-dimensional relief and visual interest. The top two floors are designed as maisonettes, a successful formula reapplied.

ADDRESS Avenida del Llano Castellano, 28034 Madrid
CLIENT Instituto de la Vivienda de Madrid
TECHNICAL ARCHITECT Carmela Amoros Prados
STRUCTURAL ENGINEER Alfonso del Rio
AREA 16,000 square metres COST 700 million pesetas
METRO Begoña (line 8) BUS 125, 135
ACCESS none

Sebastián Araujo and Jaime Nadal 1993–95

Sebastián Araujo and Jaime Nadal 1993–95

RENFE Maintenance Department Headquarters

The freestanding rail-side pavilion is the head office of RENFE's maintenance department. The project extends a smaller concrete-frame two-storey building with two further steel-framed floors of office space, built around an atrium. The upper floors are fully glazed on three sides, giving unobstructed views of passing trains. The remainder of the building is clad in sleek, silver-profiled aluminium punctured by regularly placed windows – a design totally in keeping with the concept of modern railways and modern engineering.

Vertical circulation is expressed on the south elevation by a protruding box, vertical slot window and overhanging lift machinery room. Joints between aluminium cladding panels are left open around the machinery room to allow for ventilation. The entrance to the offices adjacent to the core is defined by a simple steel canopy.

Abalos and Herreros' architecture ruthlessly adopts the machine aesthetic in its functional expressionism, offering a complete contrast to the more traditional brick and render buildings designed by most Madrileño architects. Their administrative building for the Academia Nacional de Policia (1992, Carretera de Canillas 53, 28033 Madrid) extends the language of sleek silver and mirrored glass façades. It is best seen from the Centro Comercial on Gran Via de Hortaleza; tight security makes it almost impossible to get closer.

ADDRESS Calle Antonio Gabezon, Fuencarral, 28034 Madrid
CLIENT RENFE
AREA 5000 square metres COST 31 million pesetas
METRO *cercanía* to Fuencarral (C1)
ACCESS none

Iñaki Abalos and Juan Herreros 1990–92

Iñaki Abalos and Juan Herreros 1990–92

Avenida de la Ilustracion

The six-lane Avenida de la Ilustracion was developed to connect northern parts of the city with the M30 circular motorway. Like so many motorway schemes, it was highly controversial. Junquera/Pérez-Pita were commissioned to lessen the impact of the road on the surrounding environment.

On either side of the freeway are pedestrian walkways, 18 metres wide and lined with plane trees. The large scale of the landscaping elements has been designed to suit the scale of the road and traffic. In time, the trees will grow to provide shade and a noise-insulating barrier, though currently the traffic fumes do not encourage a leisurely *paseo*.

At three points along the avenue, roundabouts slow down traffic and knit together the *barrios* on either side of the road. Originally, these nodes were cobbled but this proved too effective in slowing the traffic – they are now tarmac. Subsequently, the motorway was taken beneath two of the roundabouts, emerging only at Glorieta Las Reales Academias. As motorists sweat in jams approaching this junction they can contemplate the diminishing concentric stainless steel arches designed by the artist Alsaro. Divided to span both directions, the sculpture offers a real sense of entry and exit to the city as well as providing a local landmark.

A forthcoming architectural highlight in this area will be Andrés Perea Ortega's Fuencarral Library, due for completion in 1977 (Calle de Alfredo Marquené/Calle San Genjo, 28034 Madrid).

ADDRESS Avenida de la Ilustracion/Paseo de la Vaguada, 28034 Madrid
CLIENT Ministerio de Obras Publicas y Urbanismo (MOPU)
CIVIL ENGINEERS José Antonio Fernandez Ordoñez and
Julio Martínez Calzón
METRO Barrio del Pilar, Herrera Oria (line 9) BUS 67, 83, 124, 133, 134
ACCESS open

Jerónimo Junquera and Estanislao Pérez-Pita 1987

Jerónimo Junquera and Estanislao Pérez-Pita 1987

La Vaguada Civic Centre

Surrounded by high-rise housing, the Parque de la Vaguada mixes rigorous landscape layouts with an informal central area. This compositional interplay is also apparent in the collection of buildings which make up the civic centre at the east end of the park.

The Catalan architects Parcerisas and San José were chosen for the project following a competition in 1982, shortly after they had completed their training in Barcelona. A theatre, library, covered swimming pool, old people's day centre, health centre and local authority offices are arranged in an L-shape around a pool of water. The elements are linked by a brick-arched arcade, like an Arab hypostyle. The library and swimming pool are set beneath the arches, their expressive roofs protruding into the plaza above in a manner reminiscent of Le Corbusier's designs for the government buildings in Chandigarh.

The health centre and local authority offices are set at 90 degrees to the arcade, closing off views of the pool from Avenida de Montforte de Lemos. The arris end of the building looks like the prow of a boat, especially when seen with the sails on top of La Vaguada shopping centre behind. The predominantly brick façades and copper roofs help tie the elements into a cohesive composition despite occasional mismatched detailing, at one moment classical and the next distinctly modern.

ADDRESS Avenida de Monforte de Lemos (next to La Vaguada Centro Comercial), 28029 Madrid
CLIENT Ayuntamiento de Madrid
METRO Barrio del Pilar (line 9) BUS 83, 128, 132
ACCESS theatre: Monday and Tuesday 17.00–20.30; Wednesday to Sunday 12.00–4.00, 17.00–20.30. Library: Monday to Friday 8.30–14.30, 15.00–21.00

Jordi Parcerisas and Javier San José 1982–89

Jordi Parcerisas and Javier San José 1982–89

Cena del Señor Church

In a pioneering housing *barrio*, this unashamedly modern church has become popular with progressive church-going locals. The brief called for a variety of different spaces: a main nave, an independent chapel for daily use, meeting rooms and two apartments for the priests. The design by Estudio Dos (Carmen Bravo Durá and Jaime Martínez Ramos) places these elements around a shared hall. Each part has its own geometric form, both in plan and section, which slots into the central hall.

The hall follows the principle of the Roman temple or early Christian church, providing a break between the street and the worshipping space. Externally, a concrete roof sails over the smaller rooms, continuing the arcade along the street already begun by the local shopping centre. The brick wall of the shopping centre also continues beneath, independent of the roof, punctured to form an external window on to the church entrance. The main space for worship is a 10-metre diameter brick cylinder. The absence of windows helps the congregation to concentrate on prayer, while indirect sunlight floods down the walls to light the nave, giving warmth to the interior. The lack of detail creates a sense of piety, while the lowered ceiling over the pews adds intimacy.

Apart from timber doors, seats and altars, the finishes are low key and low budget – terrazzo, brick, concrete and steel – enabling the spatial and contextual qualities of the architecture to shine through.

ADDRESS Calle Antonio Marchado 24, 28035 Madrid
CLIENT Parroquia Cena del Señor for the Obispado de Madrid
AREA 978 square metres COST 60 million pesetas
METRO Cuatro Caminos (lines 1, 2, 6), then bus 127 BUS 127, 132
ACCESS Monday to Friday 18.00–21.00; Sunday masses at 11.00, 12.00, 13.00, 20.00

Estudio Dos 1987–89

Estudio Dos 1987–89

Casa Hachuel

Solans, Briales and del Amo began working for Jacques Hachuel in 1983 and have developed his house over three phases. Throughout the project they have wrestled with two seemingly contradictory requirements: to provide a family home suitable for young children, and an exhibition space for Hachuel's quite extraordinary collection of contemporary art.

The collection covers a wide range and includes pieces by Picasso, Bacon, Giacometti and Gris. Many of the pieces form part of the building, so it is difficult at times to differentiate between art and architecture – particularly since the architects have manipulated constructional elements into sculpture. A number of artists, such as Eduardo Chillida, Anthony Caro and Richard Serra, produced their works especially for the house. The graffiti at the front door, 'Now we're talking autographs, live from New York', is by Keith Haring, and the deconstructivist glass igloo in the drive is by Mario Mertz.

The fluorescent 'LOVE' resting on the roof suggests the world inside. The steel-framed house focuses on a central top-lit hall. A stair reduces in width as it climbs up to first-floor level, exaggerating perspective. The profiled aluminium handrails mimic those in Louis Kahn's Kimbell Art Gallery. At first-floor level, louvres to the rooflight cast shadows across the timber floor and a vast Keith Haring vase. The red and black steel structure celebrates its construction with clearly expressed joints and bolts. Bedrooms, dressing rooms and bathrooms are arranged around the hall. On the south side, the terrace stretches out to the sloping garden, sheltering the outdoor dining area below.

In the latest phase, rooms have been extended on the upper level, with the addition of three independent structures like tree houses, each with its own geometric form, clad in silver-coloured steel panels with pitched red steel roofs.

José Luis Solans, Pilar Briales and Ricardo del Amo 1988–90

José Luis Solans, Pilar Briales and Ricardo del Amo 1988–90

The library, sitting room, dining room and kitchen at entry level open on to terraces. The stair to the lower ground level is sturdier, made of steel and concrete. The handrail here uses a steel beam welded on uprights, continuing the constructivist theme. The lower floor is clad in grey aluminium panels with square windows on to the play area, gym and studies behind. This solidity gives strength to the base of the house and support for the steel and glass pavilion above. The art and architecture are all-encompassing and extend into the garden – which is also designed by the architects and which roots the house to its site.

ADDRESS Calle de Peguerinos 37, 28035 Madrid
CLIENT Jacques Hachuel
AREA 1200 square metres COST 400 million pesetas
METRO Ciudad Universitaria (line 6) then bus 82
ACCESS none

José Luis Solans, Pilar Briales and Ricardo del Amo 1988–90

Barajas

**Parque Conde de Orgaz
Private Housing**

Most private developments in the Parque Conde de Orgaz have been depressingly similar, characterised by commercial greed and little architectural merit. These two developments stand out from their mediocre neighbours. The most recent at Machu Pichu 43 is the more refined. The apartments are organised around a communal garden with outdoor swimming pool, tennis courts and play area. The buildings gently curve to follow the site boundaries and are lifted up on brick piers, forming a shaded arcade at ground level. Tenants can sit out on summer evenings, much as they would in the tree-lined streets closer to the city centre. The apartments – a mix of studios, one-, two- and three-bed units – are arranged along corridors. On each level the core areas are painted a different colour for easy recognition. Planning regulations did not permit development of any retail units at ground level, though there is a multipurpose gym in the east wing of the complex.

The three entrances are designed as minimal glass boxes which enclose marble-clad stairs and lift cores. The separate stairs which lead down to the underground car park were a requirement of the fire department. At each entrance, the enlightened client has placed a large artwork: *Epitaph Tomb* panels III and IV, both by Julian Schnabel, and a third piece by the Spanish geometric artist Pablo Palazuelo. The doubleheight entrance in the south-west corner is the best place to see the careful manipulation of details which has become a hallmark of Bayón's brand of minimalism.

The façades are well composed and proportioned, with the tautly curved, pale brick skin animated by a modern steel and glass version of the *mirador*, the protruding glass bay which adorns so much nineteenth-century Spanish urban housing. Bayón acknowledges the influence of

Mariano Bayón and Antonio Cavero 1992–95

Mariano Bayón and Antonio Cavero 1992–95

Bruno Taut, the Italian rationalists and Alejandro de la Sota, the father of the current Madrid school. This project also shows strong references to traditional Spanish architectural devices and is a clear example of how well some Spanish architects have learnt to place modernism within a cultural and historical context.

ADDRESS Avenida del Papa Negro 20–22 (phase 1, 1992–94); Calle Machu Pichu 43 (phase 2, 1993–95); Parque Conde de Orgaz, 28043 Madrid
CLIENT Cia. Urbanizadora Del Coto SA
TECHNICAL ARCHITECTS José Angel Azañedo and Juan José Delgado
SIZE 184 units (phase 1); 162 units (phase 2)
COST 1500 million pesetas each phase
METRO Arturo Soria (line 4), then bus 122
ACCESS none

Barajas

Mariano Bayón and Antonio Cavero 1992–95

Mariano Bayón and Antonio Cavero 1992–95

Parque Juan Carlos I

Sandwiched between the city, the airport and barren countryside, the park suffers from poor public transport access, with just one bus serving it and the neighbouring Campo de las Naciones.

A grove of 100-year-old olive trees has been preserved as the centrepiece of the park. It is surrounded by a 3-kilometre circular path which is in turn cut across by a freeform artificial river. These elements form the basis of the park, creating boundaries and reference points and juxtaposing hard and soft surfaces.

Within this framework there exists a variety of micro-landscapes, ranging from lawns, pyramidal hills and paved plazas to olive groves, rough pastures and beds of herbs. Running through the park like blood through veins are myriad water features: canals, rivers, lakes, geysers, spouts, fountains and waterfalls.

Sculptural and architectonic interventions add form and contrast. The consistent palette of reinforced concrete and oxidised and galvanised steel used for bridges, plazas, balustrades and monuments ties the spaces together visually and creates a strangely appealing sense of post-industrial desolation.

On summer evenings the park is floodlit, and there are cybernetic water displays in front of the amphitheatre. Designed by Antonio Fernandez Alba in 1992, this amphitheatre reveals a stern, muscular architecture consistent with the language established by Esteras and Esteban.

There are 15 major pieces of sculpture installed in the park. Among the most instantly recognisable are the three oxidised steel beams of Jorge du Bon's *Viga* (1938); the moulded landscape entitled *Paisaje Azul* by Alexandru Arghira (1935); the cantilevered concertina *Fisicromia para Madrid* (1923, Carlos Cruz Diez); and the reflective hemisphere *My Sky Hole/Madrid* (1930, Bukichi Inoue).

Emilio Esteras and José Luís Esteban 1989–92

Barajas

Emilio Esteras and José Luís Esteban 1989–92

Towards the middle of the park the ground rises steeply to form a sloping granite-cobbled plaza, the Espacio de Mexico. This was financed by the people of Mexico City as a gift to Madrid.

The park is so large that it is easy to find plenty of quiet, shady and undisturbed spots from which to survey the city unfolding to the south-west.

ADDRESS Campo de las Naciones, 28042 Madrid
CLIENT Ayuntamiento de Madrid and Empresa Municipal Campo de las Naciones SA
AREA 160 hectares COST 7000 million pesetas
METRO Arturo Soria (line 4) then bus 122 or Canillejas (line 5)
BUS 101, 105, 122
ACCESS daily May to September 10.00–22.00; October to April 10.00–20.00

Emilio Esteras and José Luís Esteban 1989–92

Emilio Esteras and José Luís Esteban 1989–92

Palacio Municipal de Congresos

The height of the conference centre was restricted to 27.5 metres due to the proximity of Barajas airport. The building therefore fills the site, enclosed by minimal elevations of striped planar glazing fixed to vertical steel trusses with corners clad in 'Giallo Dorato' limestone. The stone is etched with the relief of a neo-classical window – a typical Bofill detail which evokes the Roman ruins at Petra.

Bofill's recent architecture is renowned for its fusion of high-tech and classical references. The architects explain that the history of architecture is thousands of years old, yet the last 60 years have seen great advances in building technology. The studio's designs therefore pay homage to history while exploring technology to suit modern building briefs.

Ghost-like shadows of the interior appear through the striated glazing. Entrances through clear glass doors are weak, but the power returns on the inside.

The interior is organised around a series of independent buildings separated by atrium spaces, seen by the architects as an 'urban structure of streets and squares'. Two side buildings contain a range of restaurants, bars, offices and meeting rooms.

The vast central triangular prism contains the two conference halls, one on top of the other. Sunk below ground, the lower Auditorio América has a 1500-seat capacity, while the upper Auditorio Europa has seating for 2200. At its apex, the triangle slices through the glass skin to form a small balcony looking on to Calle Amberes.

Above the Auditorio Europa there is a multi-purpose space set beneath gently arched steel trusses; skylights fill this space with sunshine. It is directly connected to the ground floor by escalators and four marble-clad stair and lift towers.

Bofill's design is typically grandiose: precast concrete ionic columns,

Ricardo Bofill Taller de Arquitectura 1991–93

Barajas

Ricardo Bofill Taller de Arquitectura 1991–93

quarry loads of marble, inlaid sycamore veneers, full-grown palm trees and balconies spewing greenery.

The APOT building (1993–94) opposite the conference centre was also designed by Bofill. It contains 22,000 square metres of office space. The glazed curtain wall to the triumphal staircase and escalator has open vents which enable the air to move freely. The fire department considered it open space and so exempted it from fire regulations.

ADDRESS Avenida Capital de España Madrid, Campo de las Naciones, 28042, Madrid
CLIENT Ayuntamiento de Madrid
STRUCTURAL ENGINEERS Ove Arup and Partners
ACOUSTICS Xu Acoustics
AREA 72,000 square metres COST 15,000 million pesetas
METRO Arturo Soria (line 4), then bus 122
ACCESS café open

Ricardo Bofill Taller de Arquitectura 1991–93

Ricardo Bofill Taller de Arquitectura 1991–93

Juan Carlos I Trade Fair

Madrid's trade fair was moved to its current location near the airport when it had outgrown its previous home in the Casa del Campo (1965, Francisco Cabrero). The site hosts a huge variety of events, including International Fashion Week, International Leather Week and ARCO, one of Europe's most important contemporary art fairs.

Junquera/Pérez-Pita's masterplan separated operational, exhibition and pedestrian elements, placing the main service building to the west, adjacent to the M40 slip road. The eight exhibition sheds are plain, large-span steel-clad shells without scale or relief. The central avenue, by comparison, is broken down by a series of tree-shaded courtyards, arcades and brick pavilions housing retail units, information offices, restaurants and walkways. A canopy supported on slender columns forms a *porte-cochère* to the sheds. Beneath it are linear brick pavilions, cut back to form entrances to the exhibition halls and swelling forwards elsewhere to create a series of constantly varied, human-scaled spaces.

Deliveries are made to the long operational building which is divided by a top-lit internal access road. The rooflight is lifted above the roof level to allow exhaust fumes to escape. At the head of the operational building the site's air-conditioning plant is in a semicircular pavilion. The silver machinery is clearly visible behind a stepped, glazed façade.

ADDRESS Parque Ferial Juan Carlos I, 28042 Madrid
CLIENT Recintos Feriales Madrileños SA
TECHNICAL ARCHITECTS Antonio Rodríguez, Fernando Vasco and Lucinio Pérez
AREA 100,000 square metres COST 25,000 million pesetas
METRO Arturo Soria (line 4), then bus 122
ACCESS on exhibition days only

Barajas

Jerónimo Junquera and Estanislao Pérez-Pita 1989–91

Barajas

Central Pavilion, Juan Carlos I Trade Fair

Sáenz de Oíza tied with Junquera/Pérez-Pita in the competition to design Madrid's trade fair. While the latter were commissioned for the majority of the work (see page 276), Sáenz de Oíza was retained to design the main entrance and administration building. It is organised around a circular courtyard and dominated by a confection of garish colours.

The offices are lifted up on columns, freeing the ground floor for the reception of visitors and circulation through the courtyard into the fair. Cores are positioned at the four corners, popping up at roof level with yellow-framed rooflights. The outer glass skin is independent of the inner, creating an acclimatised zone for reception and a weather screen to offices above. Rooflights between building and skin complete the wrapping. The void is filled with maintenance walkways and structural space frames. All the parts are colour-coded: glazing profiles are green, space frames are white, secondary metalwork is red and the ring beam between the glass façade and the slate base is blue. Add to all this green-tinted glass and lime spandrel panels and the result is architecture's answer to pop art.

The technology application is uninspiring, the sense of entry is minimal, there is no elevational hierarchy (despite the strong north–south axis), and the colour-coding is frankly trite. This is all rather surprising because Sáenz de Oiza has been one of the prime movers of the Madrileño architectural scene over the last 30 years, creating such seminal buildings as Torres Blancas (1968) and the Banco de Bilbao y Vizcaya (1971–80).

ADDRESS Pabellon Central, Recinto Ferial Juan Carlos 1, 28042 Madrid
CLIENT IFEMA
METRO Arturo Soria (line 4), then bus 122
ACCESS on exhibition days, to ground floor only

Francisco Sáenz de Oíza 1986–89

Barajas

Francisco Sáenz de Oíza 1986–89

Madrid Athletics Stadium

The stadium is approached on foot across a grid of unnamed streets laid out for the next wave of housing developments. It is an approach that gives a clear sense of being on the very edge of the city.

The stadium is the centrepiece of a competition-winning design for a 'sports city', though to date it is the only part of the scheme to have been built. It was inaugurated just before the socialist regional government was ousted from power in 1995.

The central component of the masterplan is the 36 x 36 metre platform constructed over the service areas. The supporting walls of the grandstand rest on the platform and all the other sports facilities will eventually relate to this plaza. The nine rectangular louvred rooflights set across the platform allow light to filter through to the two levels of dressing rooms, indoor practice areas, press rooms, offices and VIP suites beneath.

The athletic track is sunk 10 metres below the platform, with the lower tier of the grandstand set into the slope, housing 8000 spectators. The remaining sloping grassy banks of the stadium are unused, though there are plans to provide a further 25,000 seats if and when Madrid secures a major sporting event.

The dramatic upper grandstand dominates the complex and has a capacity for a further 12,500. Shaped like an inclined plate, it is supported by a ring beam, with the stepped seating cast in between. It appears to hover over the series of tautly curved concrete walls which mark the edge of the platform. Seen from the side, the extent of the cantilever is exposed as a clever visual deception.

The concrete walls are pierced by the entrances and by bands of slots which let shafts of light penetrate to the stairs, balconies and access streets behind. The sculptural impact, occasional asymmetry and changing perspective of the curved walls provide constant visual interest both from

Barajas

Antonio Cruz and Antonio Ortiz 1990–94

Antonio Cruz and Antonio Ortiz 1990–94

the front and from the side. The structure has been designed to allow for the addition of a canopy: the current exposure of seating to freezing winters and hot summers seems unnecessarily daunting.

The dynamism and strength of the grandstand are also apparent in the tilted lighting gantries which hang out towards the athletics track, the lights suspended within galvanised steel frames. Unfortunately, the only breakable material in the entire scheme – the glass blocks set into the ticket booths – has been systematically smashed by vandals.

ADDRESS Avenida los Arcentales, 28037 Madrid
CLIENT Comunidad de Madrid
TECHNICAL ARCHITECTS Manuel Delgado and Fernando Vasco
STRUCTURAL ENGINEER Julio Martínez Calzón
AREA 50,000 square metres COST 5620 million pesetas
METRO Las Musas (line 7) BUS 28, 48, 286, 288
ACCESS inside only when an event is on; outside accessible

Antonio Cruz and Antonio Ortiz 1990–94

Barajas

Barajas

Antonio Cruz and Antonio Ortiz 1990–94

Telefónica Offices

These buildings, humming with the sound of machinery, serve two functions. One of the four blocks controls the telephone network for the *barrio* of Simancas, while in the others Telefónica's notoriously expensive phone bills are processed. Technicians visit two of the buildings only occasionally, leaving them unattended most of the time, a sci-fi world where people play little part.

Larrucea won the competition for the complex with a design that adopts an urban approach, breaking the bulk into fragments. The circular block facing on to Calle Julian Camarillo orientates the trapezoidal site. It contains offices and staff facilities. A sloping garden falls way from high-security entrance kiosks to the solid cylindrical base which contains the café and reception area. A glazed first floor is set back, emphasising the contrast between office and ancillary spaces. The cylinder is connected to the neighbouring rectilinear block which is occupied by a mixture of machines and offices, helping to humanise the garden entrance.

The buildings are clad in glass-reinforced concrete, matt-green Robertson panels and tinted glazing. Façades are animated by neatly detailed stainless steel walkways which shade offices and give access for maintenance. The rectilinear buildings are linked by service zones clad in punctured, anodised aluminium. The holes assist air circulation around the plant.

ADDRESS Calle Julian Camarillo 8, 28037 Madrid
CLIENT Telefónica de España SA
AREA 62,000 sqùare metres COST 7000 million pesetas
METRO Ciudad Lineal (line 5) BUS 4, 38, 109
ACCESS none

Barajas

Francisco Larrucea 1994

Francisco Larrucea 1994

Tres Cantos to San Sebastian de los Reyes

Tres Cantos Station

This commuter station formed part of a competition-winning scheme that included a shopping centre, as yet unbuilt. The change in level between the street and the raised platforms has been convincingly managed, giving a civic scale to the side of the building facing into town, and a simple single-storey elevation on to the railway.

The architects have emphasised the change in scale by covering the station building with a laminated timber monopitch roof rising to the south-east. A curved arcade supported on elegant concrete columns creates a plaza in front of the station, with an abstract sculptural brick clocktower signalling the entrance. The triple-height ticket hall leads to an underpass with ramped access to platforms. Clerestory glazing set into the east elevation allows daylight to filter into the ticket hall and reach the processional staircase which climbs up to the café and waiting rooms. A glass screen separates this staircase from external stairs which curve on one side to follow the arcade. These were to have led to the shopping centre, but now end in a terrace looking out towards the mountains.

Detailing is of an exceptional standard. The concrete columns contrast with the warmth of the timber roof and pale brick cladding. Rainwater pipes are set expressively into brick reveals, and brick panels are separated from the zinc roof by glazed surrounds.

ADDRESS Ronda de la Luna, Plaza Estación, Tres Cantos, 28760 Madrid
CLIENT Tres Cantos SA
TECHNICAL ARCHITECTS M Rodríguez-Torices, J Aguilera and
M Beotas Lalaguna
AREA 1753 square metres COST 175 million pesetas
METRO *cercanía* to Tres Cantos (C1)
ACCESS 5.45–23.30 daily

Alas Casariego Arquitectos 1986–90

Alas Casariego Arquitectos 1986–90

Ayuntamiento Offices

The new town of Tres Cantos was developed to provide inexpensive homes and commercial space in the face of rising land costs in the capital. The development has been a victim of its own success, and rents are now comparable to those in the city. The town is organised in distinct zones: industrial estates and business parks guard the flanks, with housing and retail areas along the central axis. Wide roads bordered by bland three-storey offices and plain housing schemes create an air of desolation.

This building turns its back on a barren site to focus in on itself. Elevations are clad in prefabricated white concrete panels with a minimal arrangement of square and strip windows. The armoured skin protects the building from solar penetration, wind and the fragmented urban environment. Internally, the shell has been split to reveal inner glazed walls facing across a shallow pool of water. The two blocks of offices on either side are held together by a glass lift. Bridges connect both sides at ground and second-floor levels. At one end, a lightweight steel escape stair appears stretched between the glass skins.

The organisation allows for multiple tenancies, but in fact the building is wholly occupied by the Ayuntamiento de Tres Cantos (the local council) whose staff use the double-entry lift to cross from one side to the other.

ADDRESS Plaza de las Once Colmenas 1, Tres Cantos, 28760 Madrid
CLIENT Tres Cantos SA
TECHNICAL ARCHITECT Julio Hernanz
SERVICES ENGINEERS Juan Manuel Espinosa and Juan Izquierdo
AREA 5401 square metres COST 588 million pesetas
METRO *cercanía* to Tres Cantos (C1) BUS 712, 713, 827 (líneas interurbanas)
ACCESS Monday to Friday 9.30–13.30

Andrés Perea Ortega 1990–92

Tres Cantos to San Sebastian de los Reyes

Santa Teresa de Jesús Church

This project reflects the changing role of the church through an organic, flexible and introverted design which signals itself more by understatement than by authoritarian architecture.

The building overlooks the Parque Central, which separates the commercial and residential sectors of Tres Cantos. Externally, it presents a strong wall clad in prefabricated panels of white concrete. Windows relate to the functions of the spaces behind rather than the surrounding environment. The walls undulate, their height also dependent on the spaces behind. The only element that breaks up this protective skin is the glazed crest of a skylight which thrusts up like a glass spire, indicating the temple space below.

The internal organisation emphasises the hierarchy of space, creating a delightful transition from public to private, congregational to familiar. The marriage of light and volume is especially serene. The main toplit entrance is off a garden at the west end. A conference room faces through a glazed screen into the hall, while the pews turn their back on it, looking instead towards the altar which is bathed in light from the skylight above. Beyond these more public spaces the hall emerges into a cloister, focusing on a small garden surrounded by curved glazing. The stepped roof slopes down to this garden, emphasising the introspection and human scale of the space and enabling light to filter into the heart of the building.

Internally, the ceiling of the cloister follows the roof, allowing for a balcony at first-floor level. Seminar and meeting rooms, offices and vestry are arranged around the cloister with priests' apartments above, reached by a discreet timber stair. An entrance set into the external wall gives independent access to the cloister and stair.

The detailing – slender concrete columns, clean white spaces and invisibly framed glazing – has a Scandinavian flavour, though the architectural

Andrés Perea Ortega 1986–91

Andrés Perea Ortega 1986–91

philosophy is unmistakably Spanish. The creation of spaces that are fortress-like and introverted yet fluid is repeated by Perea in many of his other projects, including the nearby Ayuntamiento offices (see page 290) and the Health Centre at El Bercial (1993, Avenida del Parque, Getafe, 28905 Madrid).

In the residential sector to the north of the church one can see the housing scheme designed by Enrique Alvarez-Sala, Carlos Rubio Carvajal and César Ruíz-Larrea (Calle Maliciosa 32, 1989) for Larcovi SA. The architects have broken the bulk of the block by dividing it into three towers and peeling away the façades to create a constantly varied composition, a recurring theme in their work.

ADDRESS Sector Pintores 11, Tres Cantos, 28760 Madrid
CLIENT Arzobispado de Madrid-Alcala
TECHNICAL ARCHITECTS Julio Hernanz and Pedro Tirado
AREA 1527 square metres COST 158 million pesetas
METRO *cercanía* to Tres Cantos (C1) then bus 713
BUS 712, 713, 716, 723, 827 (líneas interurbanas)
ACCESS office open Monday to Friday 18.00–20.00; Sunday masses at 10.00–13.00, 19.00–20.00

Andrés Perea Ortega 1986-91

Tres Cantos to San Sebastian de los Reyes

Andrés Perea Ortega 1986–91

Red Eléctrica Control Centre

High-voltage electrical distribution for central Spain is controlled from this three-storey pavilion. The circular form envelops the control room, which is the heart of the building and around which cellular and open-plan offices are arranged. This nucleus contains distribution circuits and computer controls. Every element is linked to the electrical network by microwave signals, hence the control boxes and steel antennae dotted around the lawns outside.

With its corroded look and post-industrial connotations, the Coreten steel used as a cladding material is unusual in a technological business park such as this. The contrast between the rusted steel and the dark glazing and green grass gives greater depth to the elevation than would a reflective metal panel. A secondary layer of glazing on the south elevation reduces solar heat gain and direct glare from the midday sun.

Security at this nerve centre is extremely tight. There is no direct fire escape at ground level, only an axe to break the glass. At first-floor level the escape stair is hoisted up, to be lowered in an emergency with electric controls which emphasise the machine-like quality of the architecture.

ADDRESS Calle Marconi/Calle Newton, Parque Tecnológico, Tres Cantos, 28033 Madrid
CLIENT Red Eléctrica de España SA
STRUCTURAL ENGINEER Alfonso del Rio
MECHANICAL AND ELECTRICAL ENGINEER Rafael Urculo
AREA 3500 square metres COST 400 million pesetas
METRO *cercanía* to Tres Cantos (C1) then bus 712
BUS 712, 713, 716, 827 (líneas interurbanas)
ACCESS none

Sebastián Araujo and Jaime Nadal 1991–92

Sebastián Araujo and Jaime Nadal 1991–92

Red Eléctrica Headquarters

Red Eléctrica de España was founded in 1984 to distribute electricity throughout Spain. Since then it has proved to be one of the most enlightened patrons of modern architecture, commissioning buildings by Sebastian Araujo and Jaime Nadal, Mariano Bayón, Rafael Moneo, Andrés Perea Ortega and Salvador Pérez Arroyo, alongside this competition-winning headquarters in one of Madrid's smartest suburbs.

The brief called for one of the three existing buildings on the site to be extended, a fourth three-storey building of 10,000 square metres to be constructed, and the whole complex to be unified at basement level.

The new building follows the boundaries established by the two central blocks and is clad in Brazilian 'Uba-Tuba' granite. The horizontal dimension of windows diminishes at the corners of the building as if compressed. At third-floor level, clerestory glazing is capped by a heavy aluminium fascia – a rare inelegance in Junquera/Pérez-Pita's work. The east façade, facing the existing buildings, has an outer screen of curved glazing which protects the entrance and visually binds the four buildings together. Glass to the screen is structurally silicone-bonded to aluminium channels, screw-fixed to the primary steel frame. This frame is hung from the top beam and tied back to columns with spindly steel arms which move to enable deflection under wind load.

The size of the new building dictated the introduction of a central courtyard. This is an irregular glass prism constructed exactly as the curved glazed screen. At ground level, the floor slab is continuous, but on the first and second levels it is cut back to leave a triple-height space around the perimeter of the courtyard. Each floor is designed to form a horseshoe of office space, with reception, meeting rooms and presidential offices on the east wing. Cellular offices occupy the perimeter of the horseshoe, separated from open-plan areas by a ring of circulation. Nearer the

Jerónimo Junquera and Estanislao Pérez-Pita 1991–92

Jerónimo Junquera and Estanislao Pérez-Pita 1991–92

courtyard, the compartmentalisation breaks down, allowing for an increased focus on the centre. The irregularity of the courtyard glazing creates fascinating reflections by day and the virtual disappearance of any inside-outside barrier by night.

The extended building offers a reversal of the new one: the existing central hexagon contains the control room for national distribution. This virtual bunker has been made precious by an earlier intervention by the Catalan studio Martínez-Lapeña/Torres. Triangular top-lit voids separate the hexagonal core from a ring of office space. A punctured granite screen along the south side differentiating open-plan from cellular space echoes earlier Junquera/Pérez-Pita projects for the Salamanca library (1988, Calle Azcona 42) and ENRESA (1987, Calle Emilio Vargas 7).

The complex sits on a plinth surrounded by luscious gardens looking out across farmland to the snow-capped sierra beyond. Dotted about the grounds, fluorescent tube-lights on top of thin stainless steel tubes (designed by Andrés Perea Ortega) gently blow in the wind like corn, linking the complex with its agricultural setting.

ADDRESS Paseo Conde de los Gaitanes 177, La Moraleja, Alcobendas, 28109 Madrid
CLIENT Red Eléctrica de España SA
TECHNICAL ARCHITECTS Fernando López Rodríguez and Fernando Vasco Hidalgo
STRUCTURAL ENGINEER Alfonso Gómez Gaite
SERVICES ENGINEER CIASA
AREA 25,400 square metres COST 2100 million pesetas
BUS 155 to Plaza de la Moraleja then L2, L2A
ACCESS none

Jerónimo Junquera and Estanislao Pérez-Pita 1991–92

Tres Cantos to San Sebastian de los Reyes

Jerónimo Junquera and Estanislao Pérez-Pita 1991–92

Marqués de la Valdavia Housing

In the late 1970s, the de las Casas brothers revolutionised the Madrileño architecture scene with their starkly rationalist public housing schemes in Palomeras. Their later projects continued to investigate alternative solutions, dressing buildings in render and focussing on central courtyards. In the mid 1990s the brothers split, and this is the first completed project by Manuel. Its precast-concrete cladding provides a refreshing contrast to the red brick which dominates the majority of the city's housing stock.

The development consists of a fortress wall enclosing fingers of accommodation. These in turn divide the scheme into a series of brick-paved and planted courtyards. Persevering with the theme of invention, the architect has spurned the enclosed courtyards of earlier projects to experiment with a more open, fluid organisation. The resulting external spaces are pleasant enough, but the interconnection between each dissolves the sense of focus. The façades are the same to the north and south, neglecting environmental response.

Despite these misgivings, the beautifully smooth concrete panels and the restrained proportions of the elevations have a certain power, reminiscent of the work of Le Corbusier and the Portuguese architect Alvaro Siza. Blue mosaic-tiled funnel rooflights to the parking below are arranged like sculptures in the patios and animate the development.

ADDRESS Calle Marqués de la Valdavia 141–163, Alcobendas, Madrid
CLIENT Instituto de la Vivienda de Madrid
STRUCTURAL ENGINEER José Luis Cano
AREA 19,590 square metres; 198 units COST 1265 million pesetas
BUS 153, 154 (*interurbana* from Plaza Castilla)
ACCESS none

Manuel de las Casas 1996

Tres Cantos to San Sebastian de los Reyes

Manuel de las Casas 1996

Valvanera Sports Centre

The work of Madridejos and Sancho focuses on space as the catalyst of built form. This is a principle inherited from the Basque sculptor Eduardo Chillida, whose work derives its potency as much from what is not there as from what is. Here, a rendered rectangular box faces on to the Avenida de la Sierra. Holes punched into the box cast dramatic shafts of light on to the plaster, concrete and limestone finishes.

The façades of the box are constructed independently of the concrete structure, acting as a skin to the double-height hall. This voluminous space is animated by a stepped ramp climbing up against a white concrete wall. Double-height glazing gives views from the entrance to a serene patio. The tapering volume of the patio is brought to life by a single tree, emphasising the importance of this void as the nexus of the project.

The structure of the sports hall is integral to the façades: huge steel trusses span from the concrete-clad north elevation to columns running along the top of the spectators' gallery. The roof plane stops short of the north and south elevations, stepping up to create clerestory glazing.

From the exterior the protruding glazing creates intriguing high-level views into and through the building, counterpoising the muscularity of the concrete box with an ethereal transparency.

ADDRESS Colegio Valvanera, Avenida de la Sierra, San Sebastian de los Reyes, Madrid
CLIENT Comunidad de Madrid and Ayuntamiento de San Sebastian de los Reyes
AREA 3000 square metres COST 220 million pesetas
BUS 153, 154 (*interurbana* from Plaza Castilla)
ACCESS during opening hours

Tres Cantos to San Sebastian de los Reyes

Sol Madridejos and Juan Carlos Sancho 1991–96

Sol Madridejos and Juan Carlos Sancho 1991–96

Carrillo Gymnasium

The mayor of San Sebastian de Los Reyes refers to this gymnasium and the larger sports centre on Avenida de la Sierra by the same architects (see page 304) as 'the son and the father'. A mathematician, he delights in the array of geometrical relationships within each project.

The small school gymnasium contains a multi-purpose hall and changing rooms divided by a circulation zone, glazed at both ends. In the sports centre the glazed voids protrude beyond the roof plane but in this building they are integral to the enclosure, maintaining containment. Translucent glazing set into a crisp white steel framework allows a diffuse light to fill the beech-panelled hall. The opacity of the glass concentrates attention into the space, providing a calm, introverted but spacious volume.

From the small pine-shaded public garden to the north, the combination of white-rendered façades, steel and translucent glass presents a remarkably cool vista, disguising the building's athletic function.

ADDRESS Colegio Publico Francisco Carrillo, Calle del Pilar, San Sebastian de los Reyes, Madrid
CLIENT Ayuntamiento de San Sebastian de los Reyes
COST 45 million pesetas
BUS 153, 154
ACCESS none

Sol Madridejos and Juan Carlos Sancho 1995–96

Sol Madridejos and Juan Carlos Sancho 1995–96

Index

Madrid: a guide to recent architecture

Madrid: a guide to recent architecture

Madrid: a guide to recent architecture

Madrid: a guide to recent architecture

Madrid: a guide to recent architecture

Madrid: a guide to recent architecture

Madrid: a guide to recent architecture

Madrid: a guide to recent architecture

Photographs
   The photographs on pages 131 and 187
   are by Luís Casals

Madrid: a guide to recent architecture